English Skills Practice & Apply: Grade 7

BY
DEBORAH BROADWATER

COPYRIGHT © 2000 Mark Twain Media, Inc.

ISBN 1-58037-122-1

Printing No. CD-1344

Mark Twain Media, Inc., Publishers
Distributed by Carson-Dellosa Publishing Company, Inc.

Table of Contents

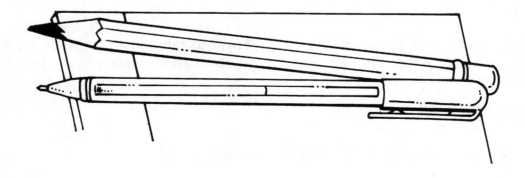

Introduction

It is important for students, especially today, to be able to communicate with others. This activity book is designed to help students by enriching their English skills. Many students do not need all of the enrichment activities in the book. The teacher must decide which activities to use to meet the needs of the students.

Each topic has a page explaining the rules for the skill and including several examples. These may be used for whole group or individual instruction. Several activities are included after each topic is discussed to provide extra practice for students who need it. Some students may understand the topic after one activity, while others may need more reinforcement. There are also writing activities included, which can be used for the application of the skills learned. A glossary has been included for easy reference of terms.

Teachers are encouraged to copy the pages of this book for use in their classrooms. The exercises will promote the ability to use the English language in writing and speaking.

Thanks to Barbara Weed for her help in writing this book.

—THE AUTHOR—

Name: _____   Date: _____

Unit 1: Nouns: *Types of Nouns Introduction*

There are four main types of nouns: **common**, **proper**, **possessive**, and **plural**.

A **common noun** names a person, place, thing, or idea.

> **Examples**: people, playground, lamp, truth

A **proper noun** names a specific person, place, or thing and should always begin with a capital letter.

> **Examples**: Laura, Florida, World Series

A **possessive noun** shows ownership. A singular noun is made to show possession by adding an apostrophe and "s" ('s).

> **Example**: Elizabeth's book

A **plural noun** means more than one. To most nouns, add "s" to form the plural. To nouns that end in "s," "sh," "ch," "ss," and "x," add "es" to form the plural. For nouns that end in "fe" or "f," change the "f" to "v" and add "es."

> **Examples**: building/buildings   class/classes   fox/foxes
>   calf/calves   knife/knives

Some nouns are **irregular** and change completely to form the plural.

> **Examples**: mouse changes to mice
>   man changes to men
>   child changes to children
>   goose changes to geese

Nouns may be formed from other parts of speech by adding a noun suffix.

> **Examples**: playful + ness   playfulness
>   patriot + ism   patriotism
>   decorate + ation   decoration
>   tolerate + ance   tolerance
>   improve + ment   improvement

Name: _____   Date: _____

Unit 1: Nouns: *Common and Proper Noun Exercise*

Directions: In the following sentences, underline the nouns. Write above each noun **P** for person, **PL** for place and **T** for thing.

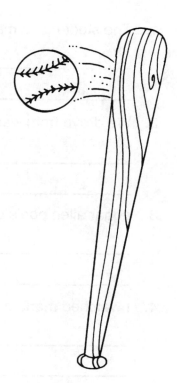

1. The small brown dog jumped on the couch.

2. Steven played on the baseball team at school.

3. The eighth grade is going to Washington, D.C.

4. President Clinton will speak on the television tonight.

5. Scientists are studying the planets of the solar system.

6. William was appointed speaker for the group.

7. Tom Sawyer is a character in a book.

8. The students use the computer in the classroom.

9. I learned to play the piano this summer.

10. My dad planted tulips in the garden.

11. Sarah is going to Florida to march in the Orange Bowl Parade.

12. The new junior high was built in 1998.

13. The kitten was a big surprise for my sister.

14. Only students write the school newspaper.

15. Have you been to the Black Hills?

Name: _____ Date: _____

Unit 1: Nouns: *Proper Nouns Exercise*

Directions: In the following sentences circle the proper nouns. On the lines below, rewrite the following sentences capitalizing the proper nouns.

1. The students at madison junior high are playing mozart at the concert.

    _____

    _____

2. We drove from washington, d.c., to mount vernon in one afternoon.

    _____

    _____

3. edgar allen poe's poem "annabelle lee" is one of my favorites.

    _____

    _____

4. I watched mark mcgwire play baseball for the cardinals.

    _____

    _____

5. Is the world series always played in october?

    _____

    _____

6. I have always liked on the banks of plum creek by laura ingalls wilder.

    _____

    _____

7. This summer we went to chicago, st. louis, and kansas city on our vacation.

    _____

    _____

8. The principal, mr. emerson, told the student council to be role models.

    _____

    _____

Name: _____ Date: _____

Unit 1: Nouns: *Plural Nouns Exercise*

Directions: Rewrite the following sentences, changing the underlined nouns from singular to plural. Underline the plural nouns in your sentence.

1. The <u>cat</u> played with the <u>ball</u> and <u>toy</u>.

   _____

2. The <u>story</u> written by the <u>student</u> will be published in the <u>newspaper</u>.

   _____

   _____

3. The <u>umpire</u> decided the <u>player</u> should be thrown out of the <u>game</u>.

   _____

   _____

4. The <u>rabbit</u> in my <u>garden</u> ate all of the <u>tomato</u>.

   _____

5. The <u>class</u> will be going to see the Indian <u>mound</u>.

   _____

6. He used the <u>match</u> from the <u>box</u> on the <u>table</u> to start the <u>fire</u>.

   _____

   _____

7. In the <u>field</u> the <u>fox</u> played with the <u>kitten</u>.

   _____

8. The <u>calf</u> followed the <u>cow</u> into the <u>barn</u>.

   _____

9. The <u>man</u> walked with the <u>child</u> to the <u>park</u>.

   _____

10. The bold <u>goose</u> waddled past the <u>moose</u>.

    _____

Name: _____　　Date: _____

Unit 1: Nouns: *Possessive Nouns Exercise*

Directions: On the lines below, rewrite the following sentences. Write the possessive form of the underlined nouns. Underline the possessives in your sentence.

1. I wore my <u>brother</u> jacket to school and left it at <u>Sarah</u>.

   _____

   _____

2. The <u>men</u> team wore blue shirts and was sponsored by Brown Hardware.

   _____

   _____

3. The <u>baskets</u> weaving was done by talented workers.

   _____

   _____

4. The <u>children</u> eyes were beginning to close as they heard the bedtime story.

   _____

   _____

5. My <u>grandmother</u> table was given to me by my <u>mother</u> aunt.

   _____

   _____

6. The <u>beaches</u> dunes looked like snow-covered hills.

   _____

   _____

7. The <u>uniform</u> coat buttons had a <u>ship</u> anchor carved on them.

   _____

   _____

8. <u>Susan</u> bicycle was left at the <u>twin</u> house.

   _____

   _____

Unit 2: Pronouns: *Personal Pronouns*

A **personal pronoun** is a word that takes the place of a noun. There are three types of personal pronouns: **subject pronouns**, **object pronouns**, and **possessive pronouns**.

The **subject pronouns** take the place of the subject. They are: **I, you, he, she, it, we,** and **they**.

The **object pronouns** are the object of the verb. They are: **me, him, her, it, us, you,** and **them**.

Possessive pronouns show ownership. Some come before the noun. They are: **my, his, her, its, our, your,** and **their**. Some are used alone. They are: **mine, his, hers, its, ours, yours,** and **theirs**.

Examples:

Subject Pronoun -   **Michael** has the highest grade average.
                         He has the highest grade average.

                         Amanda is the captain of our team.
                         She is the captain of our team.

Object Pronoun -   Ben passed the **ball** to Jeff.
                         Ben passed **it** to Jeff.

                         Mom called **Mike and Laura**.
                         Mom called **them.**

Possessive Pronoun -   **Annie's** skirt is blue.
                         Her skirt is blue.

                         Barbara's bicycle is red.
                         Her bicycle is red.

                         That is **my sweater.**
                         That is **mine.**

Name: _____ Date: _____

Unit 2: Pronouns: *Personal Pronouns Exercise*

Directions: Read the following sentences. Rewrite the sentences on the lines below, using the correct pronoun. In the space after each sentence, write **S** for subject, **O** for object, or **P** for possessive.

1. <u>Carol and Steve</u> went on the Spanish field trip. _____

   _____

2. I need to find my <u>history book</u>. _____

   _____

3. <u>Hal's</u> football team won the game. _____

   _____

4. Mom baked <u>a pan of brownies</u>. _____

   _____

5. <u>Chris, Matt, and Liz</u> have parts in the school play. _____

   _____

6. Those shoes are <u>Carol's</u>. _____

   _____

7. Where are <u>John and Jim's</u> bicycles? _____

   _____

8. Where did you put <u>the ticket</u>? _____

   _____

9. <u>The group's</u> bus arrived late. _____

   _____

10. <u>Rosa</u> will meet the girls at the mall. _____

    _____

Name: _____ Date: _____

Unit 2: Pronouns: *Object Pronouns Exercise*

Directions: In the following sentences, choose the correct pronoun from the ones given. Circle the pronoun that you choose.

1. Mike, Laura, and (I, me) walked to the arcade.

2. Just between you and (me, I), I am nervous about this test.

3. Without you and (him, he) we would have never won the game.

4. My teacher sent my mom and (I, me) a notice about the conference.

5. The bird flew right at (them, they).

6. Mrs. Brown asked (we, us) to help (she, her) with the papers.

7. Ask Jeff and (she, her) for the computer instructions.

8. (I, Me) gave (they, them) tickets to the movie.

9. Clare and Susan walked with (us, we) to the park.

10. The dolphins splashed (they, them) with water.

11. Will you come to the picnic with (we, us)?

12. John and (me, I) are going to the school play.

13. Did you see (they, them) at the mall on Saturday?

14. I wish (us, we) could have a three-day weekend soon.

15. Look at (they, them) across the street.

Unit 2: Pronouns: *Pronoun-Antecedent Agreement*

An **antecedent** is the noun that the pronoun refers to or replaces. All pronouns have antecedents. A pronoun must agree with its antecedent in number and gender. When the antecedent is singular, the pronoun must be singular; when the antecedent is plural, the pronoun must be plural. If the antecedent is male, the pronoun must be male; if the antecedent is female, the pronoun must be female.

Examples:

> **Each** of the girls has **her** own ticket.
> **Each** is the singular, female antecedent; **her** is the singular, female pronoun.
>
> **Jim** wanted to have **his** own ticket also.
> **Jim** is the singular, male antecedent; **his** is the singular, male pronoun.
>
> **We** are planning **our** summer vacation.
> **We** is the plural antecedent; **our** is the plural pronoun.
>
> **Anyone** going on Saturday needs to bring **his** or **her** permission slip.
> **Anyone** is the singular indefinite antecedent; **his** is the singular, male pronoun and **her** is the singular, female pronoun.
>
> **Laura and Annie** baked **their** first cake.
> **Laura and Annie** is the plural antecedent; **their** is the plural pronoun.
>
> **Several** people sent in **their** contest entries.
> **Several** is the plural antecedent; **their** is the plural pronoun.

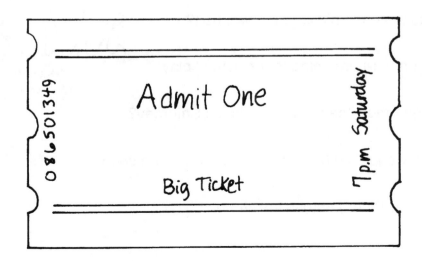

Name: _____   Date: _____

Unit 2: Pronouns: *Pronoun-Antecedent Agreement Exercise*

Directions: In the following sentences, write the correct pronoun in the blank and underline the antecedent.

1. Bill told _____ sister about the football game.

2. John and Jeff are riding _____ bicycles.

3. When Tom was baby-sitting, _____ played games with the children.

4. The cat took _____ toy under the bed.

5. Where did Allison and Jordan put _____ jackets?

6. Harry and Will have _____ lines memorized.

7. We want _____ football team to win.

8. Ask Alice to lend you _____ sweater.

9. The movie was scary; we loved _____.

10. Mike, where is _____ umbrella?

11. Chris and Steve said _____ would carry in the supplies.

12. Either Texas or Florida has grapefruit as _____ main crop.

13. Each of the boys has _____ homework finished.

14. Matt and Chris did _____ best in the race.

15. When did Mrs. Evans move _____ desk?

Unit 2: Pronouns: *Indefinite Pronouns*

Indefinite pronouns do not refer to any specific person, place, or thing. An indefinite pronoun refers generally to people, places, or things. They may take the place of a noun, but they sometimes do not have antecedents.

Some **indefinite pronouns** are:

all	any	anybody	anyone	anything
both	each	either	everybody	everyone
few	many	most	neither	nobody
none	no one	one	other	several
some	somebody	someone	something	

Examples:

Both of the books belong to Melody.

Someone left his jacket in the hall.

Neither of the girls had parts in the play.

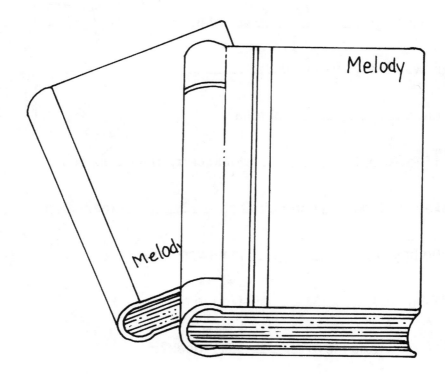

Name: _____ Date: _____

Unit 2: Pronouns: *Indefinite Pronouns Exercise*

Directions: In the following sentences, circle the indefinite pronouns.

1. Each of the students received a certificate.

2. I need both of you to carry in the furniture.

3. Would you ask a few of the art students to help with the scenery?

4. No one raised his hand to answer the question.

5. Are you going to watch either of the games tonight?

6. Would someone please pass the ketchup?

7. Carol used chalk for her drawing, but others used paint.

8. We need several students to help with the school tour.

9. I hope neither of the puppies has to be given away.

10. All of the students cheered at the pep assembly.

11. One of the elephants in the circus can stand on its back legs.

12. Everybody wanted to have an extra vacation day.

13. Where did you find some of the missing papers?

14. Most of the puppies were sleeping after they ate.

15. Does anyone want to ride on the roller coaster?

Unit 2: Pronouns: *Interrogative Pronouns*

An **interrogative pronoun** asks a question. There are five interrogative pronouns.

who　　　**whom**　　　**whose**　　　**which**　　　**what**

Examples:

　　　Who needs their paper checked?

　　　Whom have you asked to the party?

　　　Whose was the blue notebook?

　　　Which will win the race?

　　　What are you doing in here?

Hint: If an interrogative pronoun is used before a noun, it is not a pronoun but a modifier.

Examples:

What dessert did you buy at lunch?	Modifier
What did you buy at lunch?	Pronoun
Whose book do you have?	Modifier
Whose do you have?	Pronoun

Name: _____   Date: _____

Unit 2: Pronouns: *Interrogative Pronouns Exercise*

Directions: In the following sentences, underline the interrogative pronoun. Some sentences may not have interrogative pronouns.

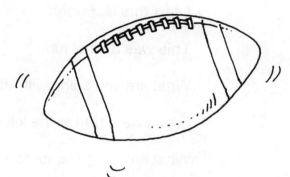

1. What are you going to do with that painting?

2. Who is riding on bus three?

3. Which is the fastest frog in the race?

4. Whose football came into our yard?

5. What dessert are you having for lunch?

6. For whom did you buy the birthday present?

7. Which notebook is yours?

8. What is the earliest you can come to my house?

9. Whom did you pick for the captain of the team?

10. Whose was the sweater in the coat closet?

11. What makes that dog run in circles?

12. What are the colors in the rainbow?

13. Who will be the next President of the United States?

14. What are you doing with that paintbrush?

15. Who turned on the water?

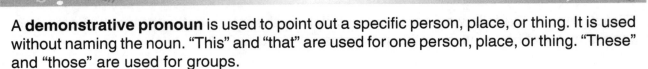

Unit 2: Pronouns: *Demonstrative Pronouns*

A **demonstrative pronoun** is used to point out a specific person, place, or thing. It is used without naming the noun. "This" and "that" are used for one person, place, or thing. "These" and "those" are used for groups.

Examples:

I saw **this** last week.

This was a lot of fun.

What are you doing with **that**?

I don't want **that** in the kitchen.

What are we going to do with **these**?

Where did you ever find **those**?

Hint: Do not use "here" or "there" with demonstrative pronouns.

Examples:

This here is mine.   Incorrect

This is mine.   Correct

I like **that there**.   Incorrect

I like **that**.   Correct

Hint: When "this," "that," "these," and "those" come before a noun, they are modifiers, not demonstrative pronouns.

Examples:

Those books fell off the shelf.   Modifier

Those fell off the shelf.   Pronoun

That oven is hot.   Modifier

That is hot.   Pronoun

Name: _____   Date: _____

Unit 2: Pronouns: *Demonstrative Pronouns Exercise*

Directions: In each of the following sentences, underline the demonstrative pronoun. Some sentences may not have demonstrative pronouns.

1. That sweater is mine.

2. This is going to be easy.

3. Those are under the table.

4. If you like mysteries, try these.

5. This was made more difficult by your refusal to cooperate.

6. I'm not sure, but I think those will work just as well.

7. Are those the shoes you are going to wear?

8. These are Jennifer's mittens.

9. This shirt is too large for me.

10. If you are thirsty, try that.

11. These papers need to be handed back.

12. I think these would be perfect for the picnic.

13. Where will you put those?

14. Whose is the blue bicycle in the front of the school?

15. Could you take this home to your parents?

17

Unit 2: Pronouns: *Relative Pronouns*

A **relative pronoun** introduces a dependent clause that modifies a noun or pronoun.

Relative pronouns are:

which	who	whose	that	whom	what

Examples:

Michael, **who** was the captain of the team, won the race.

This sweater, **which** was a birthday present, faded in the wash.

The bicycle **that** is in the garage has a flat tire.

Bill White, **whom** you met Thursday, is my brother.

Hint: Notice that some of these words are used as other types of pronouns too. Do not get them confused.

Examples:

The pencil **that** is on the floor is Carri's.   Relative Pronoun

That is her pencil.   Demonstrative Pronoun

That pencil is Carri's.   Modifier

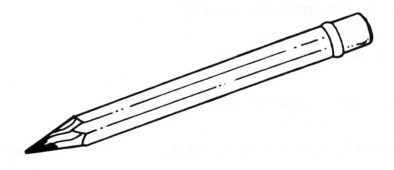

Name: _____   Date: _____

Unit 2: Pronouns: *Relative Pronouns Exercise*

Directions: In the following sentences, circle the relative pronoun and draw a line to its antecedent.

1. The clock, which has always been stopped, started to tick.

2. Ty Cobb, who was from Georgia, was a great baseball player.

3. Spaghetti, which was discovered in China by Marco Polo, has become an American favorite.

4. Michael, who goes to college, is on the fencing team.

5. The box that came in the mail was for my brother and me.

6. Calcium, which is found in milk, is necessary for good health.

7. John, who collects coins, is looking for a silver dollar.

8. The painting that hangs in the living room was painted by my grandmother.

9. This book that I bought at a tag sale is worth more money than I paid for it.

10. Stan Musial, who played for the Cardinals, had over 3,000 hits.

11. Mary, whom you met at the dance, has been my friend for six years.

12. St. Louis, which is in Missouri, is the home of the baseball Cardinals.

13. Curt, who drives race cars, came in third in the race.

14. Bill, whose bicycle was stolen, is now walking to school.

15. The dog that I got last year dug a hole under the fence.

Unit 3: Verbs: *Types of Verbs*

A **verb** is a word that shows action or a state of being about a noun or pronoun.

We **fished** at the river.	Action
Dad **mowed** the grass.	Action
Mrs. Weed **teaches** seventh grade.	Action
The cat **is** soft and cuddly.	State of being
The test **seemed** to take forever.	State of being
Taylor **is** my best friend.	State of being

There are three types of verbs: **action**, **linking**, and **helping**.

Action verbs show physical or mental action.

Michael **ran** to the bus stop.	Physical action
The dog **barked**.	Physical action
I **wish** it were Friday.	Mental action
Carol **hoped** she would win the race.	Mental action

Action verbs may or may not take objects. Action verbs that take objects are called **transitive verbs**, and action verbs that do not take objects are called **intransitive verbs**. An **object** is a noun or pronoun that receives the action of the verb.

Linking verbs do not show action. They link the subject to a noun or adjective in the predicate. A linking verb helps tell about the subject.

The oranges **tasted** delicious.

The sweater **feels** soft.

The weather **looked** cold.

Helping verbs help the main verb express the action or state of being.

Our bus **will** be late for school.

Bill **has** been on the phone for an hour.

The workman **should** arrive at 3:15.

20

Name: _____ Date: _____

Unit 3: Verbs: *Action Verbs Exercise 1*

Directions: In the following sentences, underline the subject and circle the action verb.

1. All of the students wrote essays.

2. Mary worried about passing the test.

3. Mike rode his bike to school every day.

4. Chris painted his bedroom green.

5. Saturday they went to the Royals baseball game.

6. The water flowed over the top of the glass.

7. Luis planted a vegetable garden for his mother.

8. The quarterback threw the football down the field.

9. The roofers nailed the shingles to the roof.

10. The dog slept quietly in front of the door.

11. Two hundred runners ran in the marathon.

12. Heather asked the teacher for a ruler.

13. Matthew took out the garbage after dinner.

14. I often eat pizza for dinner.

15. Todd worked on his computer all afternoon.

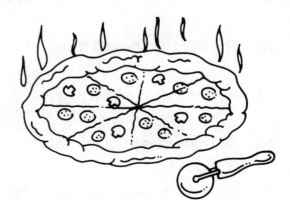

Name: _____   Date: _____

Unit 3: Verbs: *Action Verbs Exercise 2*

Directions: In the following sentences, underline the action verb and write **T** above it if it is transitive and **I** if it is intransitive.

1.   The flowers swayed in the breeze.

2.   Barbara typed her report on the computer.

3.   Bill played football all Sunday afternoon.

4.   Bob and Carol cleaned the art room tables.

5.   All the students signed the get-well card for their teacher.

6.   During thunderstorms, our dog hides.

7.   Steve thought about the test.

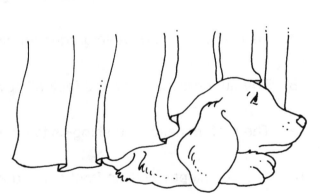

8.   Pete climbed the rock wall.

9.   We like to race to the finish line.

10.   The crowd yelled.

11.   The campers slept near the campfire.

12.   The paint ran down the picture.

13.   My sister and I share a room.

14.   The cat walked out the door.

15.   The pilot flew the plane to Chicago.

Name: _____ Date: _____

Unit 3: Verbs: *Helping Verbs Exercise*

Directions: In the following sentences, underline the helping verb once and the main verb twice.

1. I am going to the park after school.

2. My dad and I are driving to the grocery store.

3. We have gone on vacation every year for the last five years.

4. Brian has always liked chocolate chip cookies.

5. The football team has won six of its last seven games.

6. Mike has been selected to go to the student government conference.

7. Mrs. Klimstra has taken her classes to Dixon Mounds.

8. Mom will do the laundry on Saturday morning.

9. Ben has been late to school four times.

10. Stewart had asked to go first.

11. You should have come to the basketball game.

12. Those plants had grown to six feet tall before they were cut.

13. We can go to the library after school.

14. They might run for school office.

15. Would you ask for help?

Name: _____   Date: _____

Unit 3: Verbs: *Linking Verbs Exercise*

Directions: Complete each sentence below with a word from the word bank.

are	stayed	is	tasted	was	smelled
feels	looks	am	grew	were	became

1. The room _____ smaller this year.

2. The chocolate cake _____ delicious as I put it in my mouth.

3. There _____ twenty-six letters in the alphabet.

4. The temperature _____ warm for this time of year.

5. The student _____ calm during the argument.

6. The garbage _____ awful on the hot day.

7. Beth and Jane _____ late to the beginning of the movie.

8. I _____ feeling better today.

9. My brother _____ the president of the class.

10. The sky _____ cloudy before the snowstorm.

11. The baby _____ bored with the rattle.

12. Yesterday there _____ a bug crawling on the floor.

Unit 3: Verbs: *Special Verbs*

There are some verbs that are special because they have meanings that confuse people.

Set and **Sit**

Set means to place something somewhere.

Sit means to occupy a seat or rest in one place.

Examples:

Set the books on the table.   Will you **set** the groceries on the counter?

Will you **sit** closer to the door?   Will you **sit** down?

Present Tense	Past Tense	Past Participle
sit	sat	sat
set	set	set

Lie and **Lay**

Lie means to recline.

Lay means to place.

Examples:

I can **lie** down on the hammock.   Robert **lies** on the couch to watch TV.

I will **lay** my books on the table.   **Lay** your coat on the chair.

Present Tense	Past Tense	Past Participle
lie	lay	lain
lay	laid	laid

Unit 3: Verbs: *Special Verbs (continued)*

Rise and Raise

Rise means to get up or go up.

Raise means to lift or elevate.

Examples:

I will **rise** at 6:00 A.M. tomorrow morning.   Please **rise** from your seats.

You will **raise** your hand to speak.   John will **raise** the flag.

Present Tense	Past Tense	Past Participle
rise	rose	risen
raise	raised	raised

Let and Leave

Let means to permit.

Leave means to go away from.

Examples:

Let me help you with your coat.   I **let** him use my pencil.

Leave the dog alone.   You can **leave** in five minutes.

Teach and Learn

Teach means to explain.

Learn means to understand.

Examples:

Did they **teach** you the Chinese alphabet?   I can **teach** her math facts.

I can **learn** the words to the song.   Did you **learn** how to drive?

Name: _____   Date: _____

Unit 3: Verbs: *Special Verbs Exercise 1*

Directions: In the following sentences, circle the correct verb.

1. Will you (set, sit) in front with me?

2. (Let, Leave) the bicycle pump in the garage.

3. Will the bread (rise, raise) if it is left on the counter?

4. I am going to (set, sit) with my parents at the game.

5. The pets (lie, lay) on the back porch in the summer.

6. Can you (teach, learn) me how to play tennis?

7. Laura, please (set, sit) the table for dinner.

8. (Lay, Lie) your paper on the table as you come in the classroom.

9. Would you please (let, leave) the dog alone?

10. Laura will (set, sit) and read a book for hours.

11. How did you (teach, learn) all the multiplication facts so quickly?

12. I hope this accident will (teach, learn) you a lesson.

13. The students (rise, raise) their hands to answer the questions.

14. (Let, Leave) me alone.

15. I am going to (lie, lay) on the couch all afternoon.

Name: _____   Date: _____

Unit 3: Verbs: *Special Verbs Exercise 2*

Directions: In the following sentences, circle the correct form of the verb.

1. Where did you (set, sit) the newspaper when you brought it in?

2. After chasing the children, the nanny (lay, laid) down for a rest.

3. We got up long before the sun had (risen, raised).

4. Will you (let, leave) me help you with the door?

5. Mrs. Bloom (teaches, learns) English at our school.

6. The audience (sat, set) and laughed during the entire movie.

7. The dishes will (set, sit) on the table until dinnertime.

8. Someone has (lain, laid) their glass on the counter instead of the sink.

9. Carri (sets, sits) her glass collection on a high shelf.

10. The construction workers have (laid, lain) many miles of highway.

11. The barometer (rises, raises) and falls with the changing weather.

12. Sarah could not remember where she (lay, laid) the scissors.

13. The winds (raised, rose) the leaves in the grass.

14. The leaves (raised, rose) when the wind blew.

15. Make sure you have (set, sat) your watch to the correct time.

Unit 3: Verbs: *Verb Tenses*

Tense is the time expressed by a verb. Three verb tenses are **present tense**, **past tense**, and **future tense**. These are called **simple verb tenses**.

A verb in the **present tense** shows action that is happening now.
A verb in the **past tense** shows action that happened in the past.
A verb in the **future tense** shows action that will take place in the future.

Examples:

Present: I **walk** to the bus stop.

Past: I **walked** to the bus stop.

Future: I **will walk** to the bus stop.

Present: I **jump** rope.

Past: I **jumped** rope.

Future: I **will jump** rope.

Irregular Verbs: There are some special verbs that do not add "-ed" to form the past tense. The spelling of the verb changes. These are called irregular verbs.

Examples:	Present	Past
	eat	ate
	run	ran
	choose	chose
	go	went
	catch	caught
	think	thought

These are just a few. There are many others.

Name: _____   Date: _____

Unit 3: Verbs: *Verb Tenses Exercise 1*

Directions: In the following sentences, write the correct verb tense in the blank.

1. That television show _____ on tomorrow. (be - future)

2. Michael _____ the rest of the pizza for lunch. (eat - past)

3. Beth _____ to catch the baseball. (run - present)

4. Jeff _____ the team for a pep talk. (call - present)

5. Mrs. Jones _____ that newspaper story last week. (write - past)

6. Carolyn _____ to England next summer. (travel - future)

7. Cars _____ differently in the year 2310. (drive - future)

8. I _____ one dollar for lunch last year. (pay - past)

9. Our dog _____ the ball while it was still in the air. (catch - past)

10. We _____ to the movies last night. (go - past)

11. We _____ on the floor when my cousins were here. (sleep - past)

12. I _____ two quarts of water every day. (drink - present)

13. They _____ in the Mississippi River. (swim - past)

14. You _____ brownies yesterday. (make - past)

15. You _____ the dog tonight. (walk - present)

Name: _____ Date: _____

Unit 3: Verbs: *Verb Tenses Exercise 2*

Directions: In the following sentences, underline the verb, and in the space provided, write whether the verb is present, past, or future.

1. Laura asked for a pencil. _____

2. I have a brother and a sister. _____

3. Most of the people waited to cross the street. _____

4. What are you wearing to school tomorrow? _____

5. Dad cooked dinner for us last night. _____

6. Who ate all of the cookies? _____

7. I eat lunch with Susan every day. _____

8. Could I borrow your book tonight? _____

9. I am waiting for the first bell to ring for class. _____

10. My brother will go to the university next year. _____

11. I am hoping for snow tomorrow. _____

12. I wonder if we will have a test over World War II? _____

13. Stan thought he heard a noise outside his window. _____

14. My brother and I watched a scary movie last night. _____

15. How often will you walk to school this year? _____

Unit 3: Verbs: *Verb Tenses—Perfect Tense*

There are three parts to all verb tenses. There is the **present**, which is used with "to"—to go, to see, to hear, for example. There is the **past**, which shows action that happened in the past —went, saw, heard, for example. There is the **past participle**, which is used with the helping verbs "has," "have," or "had"—had gone, has seen, have heard, for example.

Present perfect tense began in the past but continues in the present or was completed in the present. You use the past participle and "have" or "has" to form the present perfect tense.

Examples:

I **have written** all the answers to the test.

She **has jogged** down that road many times.

Past perfect tense began in the past and was completed in the past. You use the past participle and "had" to form the past perfect tense.

Examples:

I **had eaten** all the pizza.

We **had decorated** the gym for the dance.

Future perfect tense begins in the future and will be completed in the future. You use the past participle and "shall have" or "will have" to form the future perfect tense.

Examples:

She **will have knitted** six sweaters by next week.

Tomorrow he **will have sat** on the billboard for six days.

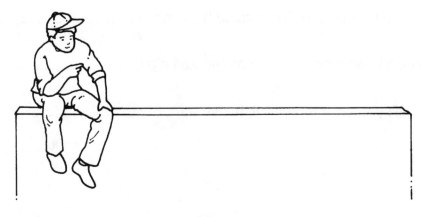

Name: _____ Date: _____

Unit 3: Verbs: *Verb Tenses–Present Perfect Exercise*

Directions: In the following sentences, fill in the blank with the present perfect form of the verb.

1. Steve _____ to school every day this year. (walk)

2. Carol _____ a letter to the editor. (write)

3. Mrs. Evans _____ me understand my lessons. (help)

4. Bill _____ the clean dishes away. (put)

5. I _____ for them after school every day this week. (wait)

6. My class _____ to London before. (travel)

7. Beth _____ squid while on vacation. (eat)

8. My dog _____ after the neighbor's cat. (ran)

9. My brother _____ six of the cookies I baked. (take)

10. We _____ all of the pens to see if they have ink. (test)

11. Carol and Jeff _____ this video on TV. (see)

12. It _____ more this year than last. (snow)

13. Mike _____ the fencing tournament. (win)

14. Our class _____ a letter from the President. (receive)

15. Chris and Matt _____ their bikes on the new trail. (ride)

Name: _____ Date: _____

Unit 3: Verbs: *Verb Tenses–Past Perfect Exercise*

Directions: In the following sentences, fill in the blank with the past perfect form of the verb.

1. After exercising, my muscles _____ for days. (ache)

2. The <u>Titanic</u> _____ before everyone got off. (sink)

3. Mrs. Garrett _____ the questions on the chalkboard. (write)

4. Laura _____ her presents early. (open)

5. William _____ to leave the class early. (ask)

6. Allison _____ the flute in fifth grade. (play)

7. Jordan _____ her mind about the job. (change)

8. Lewis _____ his neighbor with the sailboat. (help)

9. Carri _____ on her uncle's motorcycle. (ride)

10. Todd _____ the race car red and yellow. (paint)

11. In class, Curt _____ a book about model trains. (read)

12. Barb _____ a fishpond in her backyard. (build)

13. Patricia _____ to Hawaii. (travel)

14. Rusty _____ water from her water bowl. (spill)

15. Debbie _____ enough apples for a pie. (pick)

Name: _____   Date: _____

Unit 3: Verbs: *Verb Tenses–Future Perfect Exercise*

Directions: In the following sentences, fill in the blank with the future perfect form of the verb.

1. By the time I get to school, I _____ three miles today. (walk)

2. We _____ the decorations before the dance. (make)

3. Barbara _____ her project by the due date. (finish)

4. Michael _____ a lot from the chess master. (learn)

5. As a joke, they _____ matching outfits all week. (wear)

6. Scott _____ in every spelling bee at school. (participate)

7. By the end of the year, I _____ one hundred dollars. (save)

8. Jane _____ me at the end of the week who she likes. (tell)

9. Matt _____ in every classroom for his notebook. (look)

10. Laura _____ the most books in our class. (read)

11. By the end of the day, Mike _____ his room. (clean)

12. Alex _____ his piano piece many times. (practice)

13. If you eat this one too, you _____ all of my birthday treats. (eat)

Name: _____ Date: _____

Unit 3: Verbs: *Verb Tenses–Perfect Tense Review*

Directions: In the blank following the sentence, write if the verb is **present perfect**, **past perfect**, or **future perfect tense**.

1. I will have read every book in the library by the end of summer. _____

2. The action movie has broken the record for stunts in one movie. _____

3. Where have you left your coat and mittens? _____

4. Mack has gone back to get his jacket. _____

5. The dishes had been left on the counter. _____

6. Next month, Hal will have been in charge of recycling for the past two years.

   _____

7. Barb will have finished knitting the sweater by Christmas. _____

8. Have you brought the music for the party? _____

9. Brian had run that race before. _____

10. By the time you get my letter, I will have been gone two weeks. _____

11. I have been swimming since I was three years old. _____

12. Where have you put the salt and pepper? _____

13. I will have paid for all the decorations myself. _____

14. Wendy has known David for a long time. _____

15. Bill will have left on vacation by this time tomorrow. _____

Unit 4: Adjectives: *Introduction*

An **adjective** is a word that is used to modify a noun or a pronoun. An **adjective** answers the questions **what kind**, **which one**, or **how many**.

dog	**black** dog	**what kind** of dog
doughnuts	**these** doughnuts	**which** doughnuts
students	**ten** students	**how many** students

Examples:

Michael has a **black** and **yellow** bike.	what kind
Mr. Meyer has a **huge** dog.	what kind
Who needs **that** color paper?	which one
Have you ever seen **this** picture before?	which one
That kitten is hungry.	which one
We sold **some** apples.	how many
There are **two** people missing.	how many

Hint: Pronouns sometimes act as adjectives. **This**, **that**, **these**, and **those** are used as adjectives when they are followed by a noun.

Examples:

This is very good.	Pronoun
This hamburger is very good.	Adjective

Unit 4: Adjectives: *Articles, Predicate Adjectives, and Proper Adjectives*

Articles are adjectives. They are little words that come before nouns. **A**, **an**, and **the** are articles. Use **"a"** before nouns that start with a consonant sound and **"an"** before nouns that start with a vowel sound. Use **"the"** before a specific person, place, or thing.

an eagle	**a** bicycle	**an** hour	**a** test
the window	**the** flowers	**the** table	**the** chair

A **predicate adjective** follows a linking verb and describes the subject.

The team was **excited** about the win.
She was **happy** about the "A" on her test.

Proper adjectives are adjectives made from proper nouns. Every proper adjective begins with a capital letter. Proper adjectives are usually used with a common noun; you don't capitalize the common noun.

Examples:

American flag	**English** language
Spanish food	**Indian** corn
Christmas present	**Swiss** cheese

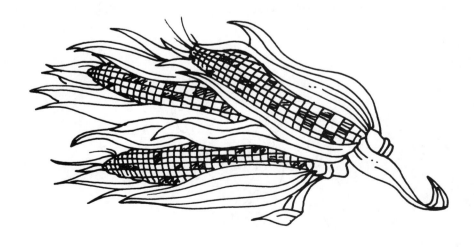

Name: _____ Date: _____

Unit 4: Adjectives: *Adjectives Exercise*

Directions: In the following sentences, underline the adjectives and draw a line from the adjective to the noun it modifies.

1. The cool air felt good after being in the hot sun.

2. After the bright sun sets, the sky turns a dark purple black.

3. Where are you going with that old, brown couch?

4. The happy students played with the antique toys.

5. May I have a large, cold glass of water?

6. Some people keep their important papers in a locked cabinet.

7. Curt took his big, black motorcycle to the two-wheeler show.

8. Beth took the yellow sweater with the pink flowers to the garage sale.

9. The tall, blue vase held long-stemmed, red roses.

10. Four chocolate chip cookies were left on the green napkin.

11. Those old newspapers can be thrown in the recycling bin.

12. While it snowed, we caught fluffy flakes in our open mouths.

13. The angry cat hissed at the big, black dog.

14. The tropical, blue water sparkled in the bright sunlight.

15. I would like to have a sandwich with American cheese for my lunch.

Name: _____ Date: _____

Unit 4: Adjectives: *Proper Adjectives Exercise*

Directions: Rewrite the following sentences capitalizing the proper adjectives. Underline the proper adjectives once and all other adjectives twice.

1. The italian newspaper reported water fountains in Rome would be turned off.

   _____

   _____

2. I would like to stay in a beautiful french chateau with a large garden.

   _____

   _____

3. Do you think that mexican food uses hot spices?

   _____

   _____

4. We saw some beautiful chinese artwork in the american museum.

   _____

   _____

5. The canadian hockey star was going to play on an american team.

   _____

   _____

6. My uncle likes german food, but I prefer to eat italian food.

   _____

   _____

7. We import irish sweaters, swiss chocolates, and english dishes.

   _____

   _____

8. The brazilian rain forests are being saved by conservation groups.

   _____

   _____

Name: _____ Date: _____

Unit 4: Adjectives: *Predicate Adjectives Exercise*

Directions: In the following sentences, underline the predicate adjective and draw a line to the word it modifies.

1. Your voice sounded sad over the telephone.

2. I was overwhelmed when they said I had won the contest.

3. The brownies smell delicious.

4. Angry dogs are dangerous to people and other animals.

5. The flowers grow tall in the warm sunshine.

6. You appear fatter on TV than in real life.

7. If the weather turns cold, we may have snow.

8. The choir sounds flat when they sing.

9. The chili tasted spicy.

10. I was tired after four games of tennis.

11. Mother remained calm as we told her about the accident.

12. Jeff looks older with a beard.

13. The bread smells wonderful.

14. Grandpa seemed happy today.

15. You are irrational in this argument.

Unit 5: Adverbs: *Introduction*

An **adverb** is a word that modifies a verb, an adjective, or another adverb. An adverb tells **how**, **when**, **where**, **how often**, and **how much** or **to what extent**. An adverb often ends in "-ly."

She answered **quietly**.	modifies verb **answered**
She answered **very** quietly.	modifies adverb **quietly**
She is **very** quiet when she answers.	modifies adjective **quiet**
Ben talked **loudly**.	modifies verb **talked**
Ben talked **really** loudly.	modifies adverb **loudly**
Ben is **really** loud when he talks.	modifies adjective **loud**
Beth asked her sister **nicely**.	**nicely** modifies the verb **asked** - how
Hal **usually** does the dishes.	**usually** modifies the verb **does** - how often
Yesterday we had a test.	**Yesterday** modifies the verb **had** - when
The clue was **clearly** visible.	**clearly** modifies the adjective **visible** - to what extent

Name: _____ Date: _____

Unit 5: Adverbs: *Adverbs Exercise*

Directions: In the following sentences, circle the adverb and draw a line to the word that it modifies.

1. The time quickly flew by.

2. The horse was very jumpy before the race.

3. I usually have my homework finished before school.

4. Paulo ran quickly up the hill to the race finish line.

5. Last year I won the speaking contest.

6. Jeanne stepped backward so the cart would not run over her toe.

7. Michael bought nearly new computer equipment.

8. Seiji always has his homework finished.

9. Yesterday our class went on a field trip.

10. Your jacket is right here.

11. Brenda very quietly went out of the classroom.

12. I greatly appreciate having the last piece of chocolate cake.

13. Have you always wanted to be a great golfer?

14. There were toys everywhere after the twins left.

15. Please turn the pages carefully.

Unit 5: Adverbs: *Using Negative Words*

Not is an adverb. When it is used with certain verbs, it can make a contraction.

Examples:

can + **not**	ca**n't**
is + **not**	is**n't**
do + **not**	do**n't**
have + **not**	have**n't**

The apostrophe takes the place of the missing letter "o." Sometimes these words are referred to as the "not" words because the word "not" is used to make the contraction.

No is another word that is used with other words to form a new word.

Examples:

no one	**nobody**	**none**	**no**	**nothing**	**nowhere**

All of these words have **"no"** in them. There is one other word that fits in this group, and that is **"never."**

All of these words together are called **negatives**. Two of these words used together make double negatives. You should avoid using double negatives.

Examples:

Sue did**n't** do **nothing** wrong	double negative
Sue did**n't** do anything wrong.	correct
Sue did **nothing** wrong.	correct
We **never** get to do **nothing**.	double negative
We **never** get to do anything.	correct
We get to do **nothing**.	correct

Unit 5: Adverbs: *Using Negatives Exercise*

Directions: In the following sentences, circle the correct word in the parentheses to make the sentences negative.

1. No one (ever, never) said you could stay up late tonight?

2. Sarah hasn't said (anything, nothing).

3. The splinter was so little you (couldn't, could) not see it.

4. You don't act (anything, nothing) like your older sister.

5. Do you want (nothing, anything) from the grocery store?

6. The kittens weren't (anywhere, nowhere) in the barn.

7. I saw (anything, nothing) that looked strange in the puzzle.

8. I (could, couldn't) not find the mistake in the knitting.

9. (Weren't, Were) none of the books on the back shelf?

10. The quiz didn't have (no, any) easy answers.

11. Haven't you (ever, never) eaten chocolate-covered ants?

12. We don't want (any, no) extra people on the committee.

13. I (couldn't, could) never learn to paint.

14. Wouldn't (nobody, anybody) join the fencing team?

15. There wasn't (no, any) money to pay for the pizzas and the ice cream.

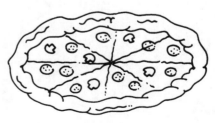

Unit 6: Adjectives and Adverbs: *Showing Comparison*

Adjectives and adverbs show comparison by adding the ending **"-er"** when two things are being compared and **"-est"** when three or more things are being compared.

Examples:

I got up **earlier** than you.

Carol is a **louder** singer than Ben.

Christopher got up the **earliest** at camp.

That was the **loudest** baby I have ever heard.

Comparison is also shown with **more**, **most**, **less**, and **least**. These are used with adjectives and adverbs that are two or more syllables long.

Examples:

Steve thinks he has the **most important** job on the council.

I take my lunch **less often** this year.

Mr. Smith is the **most helpful** teacher.

My dog is **more friendly** than yours.

Name: _____ Date: _____

Unit 6: Adjectives and Adverbs: *Comparison Adjectives Exercise*

Directions: Fill in the blank with the correct form of the adjective in parentheses.

1. My sister is _____ than yours. (tall)

2. Mrs. Cornwell has the _____ voice in the choir. (pretty)

3. This is the _____ dress I have ever seen. (beautiful)

4. My dad is _____ than my grandpa. (cautious)

5. My dog is the _____ eater. (sloppy)

6. Claudia is the _____ runner in our room. (fast)

7. This test is _____ than last week's test. (hard)

8. Steven is _____ than Jeff. (big)

9. This is the _____ day of my life. (important)

10. Jeff is the _____ boy playing basketball. (short)

11. My cat is _____ than that one. (beautiful)

12. That actor played the _____ blind person in the movie. (convincing)

13. Turn in your _____ writing assignment. (complete)

14. May I have a _____ brownie today, please? (large)

15. Where is the _____ sweater I have? (warm)

Name: _____ Date: _____

Unit 6: Adjectives and Adverbs: *Comparison Adverbs Exercise*

Directions: Fill in the blank with the correct form of the adverb in parentheses.

1. Richard can run _____ of all the track stars. (fast)

2. I completed the test _____ than my lab partner. (successfully)

3. John, you acted_____ than Jeff during the fire drill. (responsibly)

4. Louise raced _____ than Steve. (quickly)

5. My kite flew _____ today than yesterday. (high)

6. The pitcher who pitches _____ wins the game. (successfully)

7. To win the prize in speech, you must speak _____ than the other contestants. (distinctly)

8. Why do the days leading up to vacation pass _____ than the other days? (slowly)

9. Keith learned the music _____ than Robert. (easily)

10. You need to dig _____ to find water. (deep)

11. Luis read _____ this year than last. (confidently)

12. This train runs _____ than the steam engine. (speedily)

13. The bell rang _____ today than yesterday. (late)

14. My mother stays up _____ of everyone in the family. (late)

15. To win at a game, you must practice _____ of all the participants. (hard)

Unit 6: Adjectives and Adverbs: *Good, Bad, Well, and Badly*

Good and **bad** are **adjectives**. They are used to modify nouns and pronouns.

> Bill wants a **good** bicycle. (what kind)
>
> Carol's dog is a **good** dog. (what kind)
>
> I think I ate a **bad** sardine. (what kind)

Good and bad usually follow linking verbs.

Well and **badly** are **adverbs**. They modify verbs, adjectives, and other adverbs.

> My brother and sister get along **well**. (how brother and sister get along)
>
> Matt plays the violin **badly**. (how Matt plays the violin)

When talking about health, use the word **well** as an adjective.

> You look **well** today.
>
> Mom said that I am not **well** and can stay home from school.

Name: _____   Date: _____

Unit 6: Adjectives and Adverbs: *Good, Bad, Well, and Badly Exercise*

Directions: In the sentences below, circle the correct word for the sentence. In the space provided, write if it is an adjective or an adverb.

1. Beth always feels (good, well) after jogging. _____

2. Those brownies taste (good, well). _____

3. After a week, the fish tasted (bad, badly). _____

4. Carlos's CD player looks really (good, well). _____

5. Mrs. Jones said I did (good, well) on the test. _____

6. Your new spaghetti recipe tastes (bad, badly). _____

7. Sue fell and hurt her elbow (bad, badly). _____

8. Jane felt (bad, badly) about missing the appointment. _____

9. Cool water feels (good, well) on a hot day. _____

10. If you don't feel (good, well), then you should go home. _____

11. The game was played (bad, badly) and they lost. _____

12. Our team played (bad, badly) in last night's game. _____

13. You need to swim (good, well) to pass the swim test. _____

14. Peter's choice for dinner was a (good, well) one. _____

15. I hope all the plans for the dance go (good, well). _____

16. Our team ran (bad, badly) in the race, but we still won. _____

Name: _____ Date: _____

Unit 7: Prepositions: *Introduction*

A **preposition** is a word that relates the noun or pronoun that follows it to some other word in the sentence.

Examples:

We walked **to** the school.	I will wait **under** the sign.
We walked **into** the school.	I will wait **next to** the sign.
We walked **around** the school.	I will wait **behind** the sign.

The noun or pronoun used with the preposition is called the **object**. The object of the preposition usually follows the preposition.

Examples:

Matt waits near the **door**.
Near is the preposition. **Door** is the object.

Mike walked over the **pebbles**.
Over is the preposition. **Pebbles** is the object.

Barb sits in the **dugout**.
In is the preposition. **Dugout** is the object.

A **prepositional phrase** is the group of words that includes the preposition and the object.

Examples:

I waited **inside the car**.
Inside is the preposition. **Car** is the object. **Inside the car** is the prepositional phrase.

We jogged **on the beach**.
On is the preposition. **Beach** is the object. **On the beach** is the prepositional phrase.

Name: _____ Date: _____

Unit 7: Prepositions: *Object of Prepositions Exercise*

Directions: In the following sentences, circle the preposition and draw an arrow to its object.

1. My berth on the ship is below the water line.

2. I like to read about the English monarchy.

3. The waves wash over us.

4. There is a cornfield behind our house.

5. When it started to rain, I ran inside the house.

6. I received a letter from my pen pal.

7. We browsed through the book department.

8. I fixed dinner by myself.

9. My school is near the fire department.

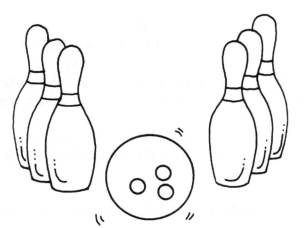

10. The bowling ball rolled between the pins.

11. The speeding car stopped against the telephone pole.

12. I would run away from a bear.

13. The picture is hung over the table.

14. I put the tulip bulbs among the evergreen bushes.

15. Nancy slid down the snowy hill.

Name: _____ Date: _____

Unit 7: Prepositions: *Prepositional Phrases Exercise*

Directions: In the following sentences, circle each prepositional phrase. Draw one line under the preposition and draw two lines under the object of the preposition in each phrase.

1. The apple in the bottom of the basket had a worm.

2. My classroom's number is over the door.

3. The racer with the fastest time will win the race.

4. The dart that lands within the bull's-eye gets the most points.

5. You must walk between the cones to pass the obstacle course.

6. I walked up the hill.

7. My dog is not to go beyond the fence.

8. My brother gave me a book of magic tricks.

9. I put the ribbon around the present.

10. The river runs toward the sea.

11. I put the bologna between the two bread slices.

12. I like to learn about American Indians.

13. I got an autograph from a famous baseball player.

14. The ball bounced near the net.

15. Check under the table for your pencil.

Unit 7: Prepositions: *Preposition or Adverb?*

Some words can be used as a **preposition** or as an **adverb**.

Examples:

The paper dropped **down**.	Adverb
The paper dropped **down** the chute.	Preposition
The boy fell **over**.	Adverb
The boy fell **over** the hurdle.	Preposition

It is important to know which way the word is used in the sentence. If the word is used alone, it is usually an adverb. Prepositions are never used alone; they always have an object.

Examples:

Phillip jumped **in**.	**In** is used alone and is an adverb.
Phillip jumped **in the pool**.	**In the pool** is a prepositional phrase.

Name: _____ Date: _____

Unit 7: Prepositions: *Preposition or Adverb? Exercise*

Directions: In the following sentences, decide if the underlined word is an adverb or a preposition, and in the space provided, write preposition or adverb.

1. I like to read <u>outside</u>. _____

2. The flower box is <u>underneath</u> the window. _____

3. Zack walked <u>out</u>. _____

4. Curt fell <u>in</u>. _____

5. They live <u>near</u> the lake. _____

6. Do you live <u>between</u> the school and my house? _____

7. Barbara worked <u>on</u> them all afternoon. _____

8. The rabbits played <u>behind</u> the bushes. _____

9. The wind blew <u>against</u> the windows. _____

10. The submarine ran <u>beneath</u> the water. _____

11. Can we run <u>across</u>? _____

12. There were people <u>throughout</u>. _____

13. Please get <u>out</u>. _____

14. The kids hung <u>around</u> the fire house. _____

15. We drove <u>along</u> the coastline. _____

Unit 7: Prepositions: *Special Uses For Prepositions*

Between and among

Use **between** when you are referring to two people or things.

Use **among** when you are referring to more than two people or things.

Examples:

I sat **between** Bill and Liz at the ball game.

There were jelly beans **among** the peanuts in the bowl.

Beside and besides

Use **beside** when you mean next to or by the side of something.

Use **besides** when you mean in addition to.

Examples:

I stood **beside** the President when I was at the White House.

I don't have much to eat **besides** a peanut butter and jelly sandwich.

At and about

Do not use **at** and **about** together.

Examples:

Sarah will arrive at 10:00.   Correct

Sarah will arrive about 10:00.   Correct

Sarah will arrive at about 10:00.   Incorrect.

At and where

Do not use **at** with **where**.

Examples:

John, **where** is it?   Correct

Could you tell me **where** it is?   Correct

John, **where** is it **at**?   Incorrect

Could you tell me **where** it is **at**? Incorrect

Unit 7: Prepositions: *Special Uses For Prepositions* (continued)

Off and Of

Do not use **off** with **of.**

Examples:

The ball rolled **off** the table.	Correct
Get the milk **off** the counter.	Correct
The ball rolled **off of** the table.	Incorrect
Get the milk **off of** the counter.	Incorrect

Of and Have

Do not use the preposition **of** for the helping verb **have**

Examples:

Beth would **have** done the work herself.	Correct
I must **have** left my mittens at school.	Correct
Beth could **of** done the work herself.	Incorrect
I must **of** left my mittens at school.	Incorrect

To

Do not add **to** if not needed.

Examples:

Where are you going?	Correct
Where are you going **to**?	Incorrect

Name: _____ Date: _____

Unit 7: Prepositions: *Special Prepositions Exercise 1*

Directions: In the following sentences, circle the correct prepositions.

1. I sat (between, among) the children when the story was read.

2. (Between, Among) you and me, I think this test will be easy.

3. (Beside, Besides) the two of us, who is going to the play?

4. Please put the crackers (beside, besides) the bread in the pantry.

5. Look at that tulip growing (between, among) the two roses.

6. The disagreement was (between, among) those three students.

7. What do you have to eat (beside, besides) peanut butter and jelly?

8. We are going to divide our money (between, among) several charities.

9. I couldn't get (between, among) the two lines in the hall.

10. I sat (beside, besides) Mr. Sanchez in the school assembly.

11. There was no one left in the classroom (beside, besides) Mrs. Jones.

12. How can you choose (between, among) all the great prizes?

13. Would you stand (between, among) Ling and Rita?

14. I found a dollar in my jeans (beside, besides) the two dollars you have.

15. Could you all get along (between, among) yourselves?

Name: _____   Date: _____

Unit 7: Prepositions: *Special Prepositions Exercise 2*

Directions: In the following sentences, circle the correct word or words that best complete each sentence.

1. The marble rolled (off, off of) the table and onto the floor.

2. Tomorrow I need to be ready to go (at about, at) 7:45.

3. Where are you taking the (package, package to)?

4. Mary (could have, could of) made the cake for the party.

5. We will be home (at, at about) 4:00.

6. I never know where I will find my (book, book at).

7. The water ran (off of, off) the new raincoat.

8. I (should of, should have) had an "A" on that paper.

9. We (could of, could have) won the game with one more run.

10. Have you seen where Jim (is, is at)?

11. The train will arrive (at about, at) 12:30.

12. The yarn rolled (off of, off) the chair and onto the floor.

13. I must (have, of) added these two numbers incorrectly.

14. I need the book; will you show me where it (is, is at)?

15. The musical starts (about, at about) 8:00.

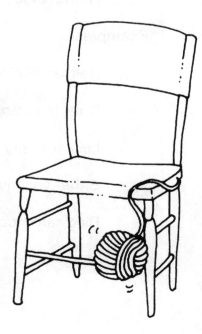

Unit 8: Conjunctions: *Types of Conjunctions*

A **conjunction** is a word that joins words or groups of words. The most common type of conjunctions are the **coordinating conjunctions**. They are used to join similar words or groups of words.

Coordinating conjunctions are:

      and   **nor**   **but**   **for**   **yet**   **so**   **or**

Examples:

> The dog looked cold **and** hungry.

> Ask Jim **or** Nancy to help.

> I will be home, **but** I will be late.

> We lost the game, **so** we were out of the tournament.

Correlative conjunctions are conjunctions that are <u>always</u> used in pairs.

Correlative conjunctions are:

     both... and   **neither...nor**   **either...or**   **whether...or**

     not only...but also

Examples:

> **Neither** Kimiko **nor** Beth read that book.

> **Both** Mom **and** Dad go to conferences.

> Luis **not only** hit a home run, but **also** hit a triple.

> **Either** you must clean your room **or** I will.

> Rico can't decide **whether** to ride the bus **or** walk to school.

Name: _____ Date: _____

Unit 8: Conjunctions: *Coordinating Conjunctions Exercise*

Directions: In the following sentences, circle each of the coordinating conjunctions and underline the word or groups of words that are joined.

1. Taylor and Allison drew pictures for the art contest.

2. I was grounded, so I couldn't talk on the phone.

3. I studied three hours, and I got an "A" on the test.

4. I needed paper, a pen, and a notebook for English class.

5. Jason or Samo will pitch today.

6. I washed and ironed the blouse.

7. I waited for Laura, but she never came to meet me.

8. Hal or Mike got to play in the game.

9. Did you like your peanut butter and jelly sandwich?

10. I have to decide to watch TV or do my homework.

11. There are fourteen books and twenty-four dictionaries on the shelves.

12. Did you ask Brian or Bill to sing?

13. Would you turn this in, for I am late to class?

14. Can you carry those boxes, or should I help you?

15. Abe, Kip, and Greta are my friends from camp.

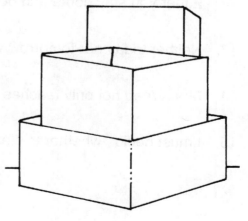

Name: _____ Date: _____

Unit 8: Conjunctions: *Correlative Conjunctions Exercise*

Directions: In the following sentences, circle each of the correlative conjunctions and underline the word or groups of words that are joined.

1. Neither Dennis nor Susan will be at the debate.

2. The dog is both scary and cute.

3. Either you will sit in your seat or you will have to sit on the floor.

4. Kathy must decide whether to baby-sit or go with her friends.

5. I not only take care of the dog but also the cat.

6. Either Barbara or Carri will make the speech.

7. My brother must decide whether to play baseball or tennis.

8. Not only Franklin but also Mateo made the honor roll.

9. I have not only a Cardinal's but also a Cub's team poster.

10. Neither my sister nor I have any money left.

11. Not only our team but our rival's team went to the state tournament.

12. Either you stay home and do homework tonight or you will have to do it Friday.

13. Neither today nor tomorrow will be a good day to stay after school.

14. Mrs. Weed not only teaches math but also history.

15. I must decide whether to clean my room or go for a walk.

Unit 9: Interjections: *Introduction*

An **interjection** is a word or phrase used to express strong or sudden feeling, emotion, or surprise. A comma or an exclamation point is used to set the interjection off from the rest of the sentence. You use an exclamation point when you want to express strong emotion and the comma when you want to express mild emotion. Notice that after the exclamation point, the next word begins with a capital because it is a new sentence.

These are some words used as interjections:

alas	great	help	hooray	never	whew
goodness	yea	hey	yippee	oh	wow

Examples:

> **Hey!** Look out below.
>
> **Stop!** Wait for me.
>
> **Wow!** Check out that bike.
>
> **Never!** I will not cheat.

Some interjections are milder.

Examples:

> **Oh,** did you say something?
>
> **Goodness,** I think I am tired.
>
> **Nonsense,** that wouldn't be any fun.

Name: _____   Date: _____

Unit 9: Interjections: *Exercise 1*

Directions: In each of the following sentence, underline the interjection.

1. Hey! Can I come too?

2. Ugh! Get that away from me.

3. Beth yelled, "Stop! Watch out for the car."

4. Well, it looks like we are finished.

5. Whew! Is it ever hot out here.

6. Grandpa said, "My, the cars are a lot faster than in my day."

7. Help! Catch me.

8. Wow! Look at the hot air balloon.

9. No way! I am not going to help with that.

10. Nonsense, you won't be late for dinner.

11. Yippee! I am going to the circus.

12. Oh, was that your book?

13. Aha! So you're the one stealing the cookies.

14. Great! I knew that science experiment wouldn't work.

15. "Never!" he yelled.

Unit 9: Interjections: *Exercise 2*

Directions: Rewrite each of the following sentences. Place an exclamation point after an interjection that has strong feeling and a comma after an interjection that is milder.

1. Great I knew you could win that race.

   _____

2. Nonsense there is no one under your bed.

   _____

3. Yea our team is number one.

   _____

4. Stop don't cross the street yet.

   _____

5. My how you have grown.

   _____

6. Help I am stuck in the elevator.

   _____

7. Ugh don't come near me with that bug.

   _____

8. Francesca yelled, "Get away don't come any closer."

   _____

9. Well I don't think the dog will hurt you.

   _____

10. Oh you shouldn't get your clothes dirty.

   _____

Unit 10: Subject and Predicate: *Introduction*

The **subject** of the sentence is the person, place, or thing that the sentence is about. The **simple subject** is just the main noun.

Examples:

My cat hid under the car.

My cat is the subject; **cat** is the simple subject.

Seventh-grade students work hard.

Seventh-grade students is the subject; **students** is the simple subject.

The **predicate** part of the sentence says something about the subject. The **simple predicate** is the verb or verb phrase.

Examples:

I rode my bike to school.

Rode my bike to school is the predicate; **rode** is the verb.

John had eaten pizza for dinner last night.

Had eaten pizza for dinner last night is the predicate; **had eaten** is the verb phrase.

The subject is not always at the beginning of the sentence.

Examples:

Sarah wrote a poem.   beginning

Writing the poem was **Sarah**.   end

A poem **Sarah** wrote.   middle

Name: _____   Date: _____

Unit 10: Subject and Predicate: *Exercise 1*

Directions: In the following sentences, underline the complete subject once and the simple subject twice. Circle the verb.

1. After the movie, we went for ice cream.

2. Six kittens played on the carpet.

3. A barking dog was behind the fence.

4. I wish I had less homework.

5. The snow fell in soft drifts.

6. During lunch we had a fire drill.

7. Watching the baseball game were the fans.

8. Did you leave your books at school?

9. Do you think this class has too many tests?

10. Oh no, I lost the recipe for the casserole.

11. On the ship were all the sailors.

12. Band practice will be held after school.

13. My sister and I are going to the mall this afternoon.

14. From the tree limb the bird watches for a worm or bug.

15. Would you please feed the dog?

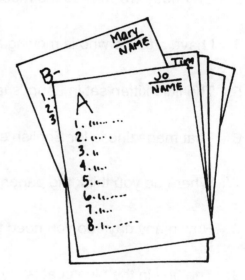

Name: _____ Date: _____

Unit 10: Subject and Predicate: *Exercise 2*

Directions: In the following sentences, underline the complete predicate. Underline the verb twice. Circle the simple subject.

1. Mary worked at the grocery store.

2. My dad helps wash the dishes.

3. On Friday we went to the museum.

4. I have a friend who is moving to Iowa.

5. The little kitten sat in Laura's lap.

6. That magazine is for English students.

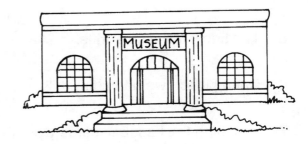

7. Where do you think the paper is?

8. How many days do you need to finish the project?

9. The boy in the blue coat is my cousin.

10. The hours in a school day move very slowly.

11. My toast fell on the floor.

12. The little girl tripped over the rug.

13. I ate four pieces of pizza.

14. Would you walk with me to the bus stop?

15. The students were working in groups.

Unit 10: Subject and Predicate: *Subject-Verb Agreement: Introduction*

The subject and verb in a sentence must **agree**. Subjects and verbs can both be **singular** or **plural**.

If the subject is singular, the verb must be singular. If the subject is plural, the verb must be plural.

If the subject is singular, add "s" to the verb. If the subject is plural, don't add an ending to the verb.

Examples:

Beth talks on the phone.	Singular subject, singular verb
Apples taste delicious.	Plural subject, plural verb
Mike and Matt play baseball	Plural subject, plural verb

Some sentences begin with "There is" or "There are." "There" is not the subject; the subject usually comes after the verb.

Examples:

There **is** a dog in our yard.	Use **is** because **dog** is singular.
There **are** six boxes on the table.	Use **are** because **boxes** is plural.

It is the same for "here" and "where."

A sentence needs both a subject and a predicate. If either one of these is missing, it is called a **sentence fragment**. If the thought of the sentence is not complete, it is also a sentence fragment.

Examples:

My dog is big and brown.	Complete sentence
My is big and brown.	Fragment (missing subject)
My dog big and brown.	Fragment (missing verb)
My dog is.	Fragment (thought not complete)

Name: _____   Date: _____

Unit 10: Subject and Predicate: *Subject-Verb Agreement: Exercise*

Directions: In the following sentences, underline the subject of the sentence, then circle the form of the verb given in the parentheses that agrees with the subject of the sentence.

1. The cats (hunts, hunt) for mice.

2. She (walks, walk) to school for exercise.

3. Mr. Ricardo (teaches, teach) Spanish.

4. An airplane (soars, soar) over our heads.

5. The dishes (is, are) in the cupboard.

6. Mrs. Yung (talks, talk) with her students every day.

7. The students (plans, plan) the carnival.

8. They (eats, eat) lunch together.

9. Here (is, are) the papers you were looking for.

10. Luis (sits, sit) in the front of the auditorium.

11. Svetlana (takes, take) piano lessons.

12. The program (is, are) not correct for the performance.

13. The dog (acts, act) friendly.

14. The cake (looks, look) delicious.

15. The dog (barks, bark) at the rabbit in the yard.

Name: _____   Date: _____

Unit 10: Subject and Predicate: *Subject-Verb Agreement With Prepositional Phrases Exercise*

Directions: In the following sentences, choose the correct form of the verb and write it in the blank.

1. The clothes in the dryer _____ dry. (is, are)

2. The cat in the window _____ sleeping. (is, are)

3. My brother in college _____ every night. (study, studies)

4. The choir of boys _____ at performances. (sings, sing)

5. The brownies from the store _____ delicious. (tastes, taste)

6. The cloths under the sink _____ for the dishes. (is, are)

7. My trunk down in the basement _____ full of sweaters. (is, are)

8. The cabinet over the stove _____ sometimes warm. (is, are)

9. The papers from the computer _____ neater. (seems, seem)

10. People in the hospital _____ care. (needs, need)

11. The donkey from the farm _____ oats. (eats, eat)

12. The envelopes in the basket _____ stamps. (needs, need)

13. The ballplayer on the team _____ every day. (practices, practice)

14. The clown at the circus _____ a tall hat. (wears, wear)

15. The piglets _____ in the barn with their mother. (sleeps, sleep)

Name: _____   Date: _____

Unit 10: **Subject and Predicate:** *Sentence Fragments Exercise*

Directions: On the following lines rewrite the sentence fragments as complete sentences.

1. after breakfast

   _____

   _____

2. Carlos and Luis

   _____

   _____

3. is beyond belief

   _____

   _____

4. that ugly shirt is

   _____

   _____

5. seven large trees fell

   _____

   _____

6. sat under a tree

   _____

   _____

7. under the bridge

   _____

   _____

8. hamburger and french fries

   _____

   _____

Unit 10: Subject and Predicate: *Combining Subjects, Predicates, and Sentences*

When writing, you sometimes have many short sentences that could go together to make your writing more interesting.

Combining Subjects

If you have two short sentences that have the same predicate, you can combine the subjects to make one sentence.

Examples:

Debbie played the piano. Laura also played the piano.

Debbie and Laura played the piano.

Combining Predicates

If you have two short sentences with the same subject, you can combine the predicates to make one sentence.

Examples:

Michael went to the park. Michael fed the ducks.

Michael went to the park and fed the ducks.

Combining Sentences

If you have two short sentences about the same topic, you can combine those to make one sentence. When you combine sentences, you need to add a comma and a conjunction like **and** or **but**.

Examples:

I like to read books. My favorite author is Mark Twain.

I like to read books, and my favorite author is Mark Twain.

Name: _____ Date: _____

Unit 10: Subject and Predicate: *Combining Subjects Exercise*

Directions: Rewrite the sentences on the lines below. Combine the subjects in each pair.

1. Steven is on the soccer team. Kevin is also on the soccer team.

   _____

2. Math is a difficult subject. Science is a difficult subject too.

   _____

3. George Washington was our President. George Bush was also our President.

   _____

   _____

4. Cindy rode her bicycle. I rode my bicycle.

   _____

5. Curt rides motorcycles for fun. Carol rides motorcycles for fun.

   _____

Directions: On the lines below, write a sentence and combine the subjects.

1. dogs and cats

   _____

   _____

2. students and teachers

   _____

   _____

3. Ben and Phillip

   _____

   _____

Name: _____ Date: _____

Unit 10: Subject and Predicate: *Combining Predicates Exercise*

Directions: On the lines below, rewrite the sentences Combine the predicates of each pair.

1. My dog chews up shoes. My dog slobbers water all over.

   _____

   _____

2. Darrel cleaned his room. Darrel vacuumed the house.

   _____

   _____

3. Wong baked chocolate chip cookies. Wong shared them with his friends.

   _____

   _____

4. My mom works at a bank. My mom drives me to school.

   _____

   _____

5. Jordan is in seventh grade. Jordan is president of the student council.

   _____

   _____

6. Keiko went to London this summer. Keiko took many pictures.

   _____

   _____

7. My dad cut the grass. My dad trimmed all the bushes.

   _____

   _____

8. Our cat howls to go outside. Our cat is afraid of birds.

   _____

Name: _____ Date: _____

Unit 10: Subject and Predicate: *Combining Sentences Exercise*

Directions: On the lines below, combine the two sentences using **and** or **but**.

1. Kareem wanted to raise birds. His mom told him it would be too messy.

   _____

   _____

2. My teacher has three computers. Two of them are very slow.

   _____

   _____

3. Mom washed the car. I washed the car windows.

   _____

   _____

4. I am going to the movies tonight. I have to take my sister with me.

   _____

   _____

5. I have a television in my room. My sister wishes she had one too.

   _____

   _____

6. Ice skating is fun to do. I usually fall down once or twice.

   _____

   _____

7. I am good in math. I have trouble with my science.

   _____

   _____

8. My dad is a great cook. I help him sometimes.

   _____

   _____

Unit 11: Clauses: *Introduction*

A **clause** is a group of words that has a subject and a verb and is used as part of a sentence.

Examples:

We raked leaves while Dad trimmed the trees.

I have a paper route because I am saving for a bike.

There are two kinds of clauses, **independent** and **dependent.**

An **independent clause** has a subject and a verb and is a complete thought.

Examples:

We raked leaves. (independent clause)

I have a paper route. (independent clause)

A **dependent clause** has a subject and a verb but is not a complete thought.

Examples:

while Dad trimmed the trees (dependent clause)

because I am saving for a bike (dependent clause)

A **dependent clause** must be with an **independent clause** to complete the meaning. The two clauses are connected with a **subordinate conjunction** or a **relative pronoun.**

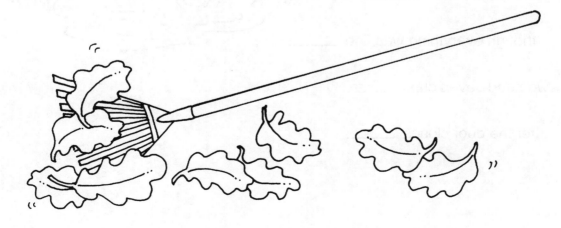

Name: _____ Date: _____

Unit 11: Clauses: *Exercise 1*

Directions: In the blank space write **I** if it is an independent clause and **D** if it is a dependent clause.

1.   I need a ride _____

2.   while the driver steered _____

3.   because it was snowing _____

4.   it is raining _____

5.   but they caught cold _____

6.   they pulled very hard _____

7.   winter is the best season _____

8.   since I walked home _____

9.   the dog ran out the door _____

10.   which is under the book _____

11.   before they finished the game _____

12.   Carol went home _____

13.   although everything was fine _____

14.   we need seven cups _____

15.   after the door closes _____

Name: _____ Date: _____

Unit 11: Clauses: *Exercise 2*

Directions: In the following sentences, underline the independent clause once and the dependent clause twice.

1. I need to find my shoes since I want to go outside.

2. Because it was snowing, the bus arrived late.

3. Chip held the dog, while Bill put on the collar.

4. Sue was sad because she didn't get the lead in the play.

5. If you don't want to come, that's all right with me.

6. Whenever you have the ball, you need to throw it to a base quickly.

7. The picture frame broke when it fell off the wall.

8. I would like to have dinner, but no one is home.

9. After you finish your dinner, you may have dessert.

10. If you get your coat, we have time to catch the bus.

11. The boy walked while the dog ran.

12. After we went to the circus, we went out for dinner.

13. Steven's dad takes us to school because it is on his way.

14. Since I was absent, I didn't have my homework ready.

15. I was absent because I had broken my hand.

Unit 12: Commas: *Introduction*

Commas are used between words to show a pause. They are also used in a series of words or ideas to keep them from running together. The comma is one of the most important punctuation marks.

Use a comma to separate items in a series of three or more.

Examples:

We saw the elephants, tigers, and lions at the zoo.

Barb, Bill, and Debbie walked to school.

Use a comma to separate the digits in a number.

Examples:

There are 1,800 students in our school.

The population of the United States is over 250,000,000.

Use a comma to join two simple sentences that are about the same thing into a **compound sentence**. Use a connecting word like "and" or "but."

Examples:

I walked to school in the rain, and I got wet.

Michael likes to use the computer, but Laura would rather read.

Use a **comma** to separate two or more adjectives in a series that modify the same noun.

Examples:

The cat had seven fat, fluffy, white kittens.

The fierce, black, big-toothed dog growled through the fence.

Hint: If you can put "and" between the adjectives and the sentence reads well, then use a comma and omit the and.

Use a comma to set off the names of someone being addressed.

Examples:

John, turn in your homework.

Mrs. Dohm, what is the answer to question six?

Unit 12: Commas: *Introduction (continued)*

Use commas to set off words that explain the noun they follow. This is called an **apposi-tive**.

Examples:

Mr. Sung, the man next door, helped me with my bike.

Brigitte, the girl with the red hair, is standing by the door.

Use commas to set off interrupting phrases that come in the middle of the sentence.

Examples:

I have, as you know, been in two school plays.

That is, if I am not mistaken, my cue to speak.

Hint: These phrases can be removed and the sentence will still make sense.

Commas are used to separate the day of the month from the year. If the date comes in the middle of the sentence, use a comma after the year.

Examples:

My birthday is February 25, 1989.

On July 4, 1776, independence was declared.

Use a comma to separate the city from a state or country. If the city and state or country come in the middle of the sentence, use a comma after the state or country name.

Examples:

St. Louis, Missouri   Quincy, Illinois

Barbara and Heidi live in Urbana, Illinois, on Chestnut Street.

My sister has lived in London, England, since 1994.

Use a comma to separate two or more introductory prepositional phrases or to set off an introductory prepositional phrase from the rest of the sentence.

Examples:

In my green coat, in the pocket, are the extra keys.

After the game, I will come straight home.

Name: _____   Date: _____

Unit 12: Commas: *Commas With Dates Exercise*

Directions: In the following sentences, add commas where they are needed. Circle the commas that you add.

1. My best friend Laura's birthday is June 11 1989.

2. We moved into our house on February 9 1992.

3. Did something important happen on December 3 1975?

4. I am going to a baseball game Thursday October 14.

5. Our class trip will be June 15 2001.

6. Did you know that July 4 1776 is an important date in history?

7. I think we get out of school Friday November 23.

8. Is January 1 2000 the start of the new millennium or January 1 2001?

9. What day of the week was March 25 1885?

10. My grandmother's anniversary is September 21 1940.

11. The levee broke on the Mississippi River on July 6 1993.

12. Pearl Harbor was attacked on Sunday December 7 1941.

13. We are going to the hockey game on Monday December 11.

14. My sister was born on Thursday January 6.

15. Thursday May 14 1992 we moved into our house.

Name: _____   Date: _____

Unit 12: Commas: *Exercise 1*

Directions: In the following sentences, add commas where they are needed. Circle the commas that you add and be ready to tell why you put them in the sentence.

1. My dad visited London Paris and Madrid when he was in Europe.

2. We all must help with recycling or we will need to build more garbage dumps.

3. Mom where do you want me to put the clean laundry?

4. Dennis the president of student council will talk to the seventh-grade class.

5. Have you ever visited Miami Florida?

6. This paper is due Thursday February 22.

7. After school I walk the dog deliver newspapers and do my homework.

8. No I am not allowed to stay out past curfew.

9. Lewis is a talented caring person.

10. That is I believe my dog running down the street.

11. I came home did my homework and went to bed.

12. The pie was golden brown warm and delicious.

13. Mrs. Stevens the school nurse gives the flu shots every year.

14. I live in Chicago Illinois.

15. Dad can I go with them to the movies?

Name: _____   Date: _____

Unit 12: Commas: *Exercise 2*

Directions: In the following sentences add commas where needed. On the line following the sentence, write why you added the commas.

1. Donna added the milk and I stirred the batter. _____

2. We had hot dogs soda peanuts and popcorn at the game. _____

3. Luella where are you? _____

4. Yes I think I can baby-sit. _____

5. Your dentist appointment is Thursday August 3 2000. _____

6. I have never been to Salt Lake City Utah. _____

7. Kansas I believe is the Sunflower State. _____

8. My neighbor Mrs. Hobbs bakes great cakes. _____

9. My cat sleeps eats and sleeps again. _____

10. I think Carlos that you would be an excellent leader. _____

11. I think I would like to visit Bangor Maine. _____

12. The moon is 239 000 miles from the earth. _____

13. My dog was born May 31 1996. _____

14. We could I suppose go one night without TV. _____

15. Mr. Williams my third-grade teacher collects old telephones. _____

Name: _____ Date: _____

Unit 12: Commas: *Independent Clause Exercise*

Directions: In the following sentences, add commas to separate the independent clauses. Circle the commas that you add.

1. I have taken three years of lessons yet I am not very good at the piano.

2. I will not take the dog out alone nor will I walk in the dark.

3. There are four papers with no name on them but none of them are mine.

4. Could I borrow your red sweater or would you rather that I didn't?

5. I washed my dad's car and I vacuumed the interior.

6. I got up early this morning but I missed the school bus.

7. No one was home nor were they expected anytime soon.

8. We can go to the store and we can buy bread for my mom.

9. I really liked the book but I thought it was very long.

10. The dog looked so innocent yet she had part of my shoe in her mouth.

11. I tried to carry the tray carefully but the plates slid off.

12. Sherry had hoped for a part in the play but she was part of the crew.

13. I want to get my homework done and I want to see the TV movie.

14. Would you like to write about a holiday or would you like to write about summer vacation?

15. Sun Li has a sister and I have a brother.

Name: _____ Date: _____

Unit 12: Commas: *Separating Dependent Clauses From Independent Clauses Exercise*

Directions: Use a comma to separate the dependent clause from the independent clause. Circle the commas you have added.

1. When I walked into my classroom I remembered we were having a test.

2. Since it was Thursday Jeff had to baby-sit his brother.

3. Until the weather gets warmer you will have to wear a coat.

4. If you want to do well on your math test you must study the lessons.

5. While you are working with the scissors please be careful.

6. Because there are twenty-seven students it is difficult to make teams of two.

7. Although I have saved my money I don't have enough for the school trip.

8. When the pond froze I got out my ice skates.

9. If you want a ride to school you need to get up earlier.

10. Until fall comes I just dream about football.

11. Because Dad travels he has many wonderful pictures.

12. After the play we went out for pizza.

13. Before we begin class we recite the Pledge of Allegiance.

14. Since Barb is so good at piano she has started giving piano lessons.

15. If you practice your musical instrument you will get better at it.

Name: _____   Date: _____

Unit 12: Commas: *Prepositional Phrases Exercise*

Directions: In the following sentences, add commas to make the sentence correct. Circle the commas you have added.

1. After dinner we all went for a walk.

2. In the middle of my sentence John interrupted.

3. Under the living room couch my homework lay.

4. After all the practices I still didn't make the football team.

5. On the corner of 12th Street and Elm Street the public library stands.

6. In the back of the classroom the goldfish bowl sat.

7. During my speech I forgot to show the graph.

8. In spite of all Karen's effort the fund raiser was a hundred dollars short.

9. With the addition of Lincoln and Kurt we will have a great team.

10. In the middle of the classroom a cart with all our dictionaries sits.

11. Across the river a small village is located.

12. During basketball time-outs the cheerleaders cheer.

13. In the morning Maria and Luis will walk to school.

14. After 10:00 P.M. my mom won't let me answer the phone.

15. At the end of the school day all the clubs meet.

Unit 13: Semicolons and Colons: *Introduction*

A **semicolon** is sometimes used in place of a comma. It indicates a longer pause than the comma.

A semicolon is used to link independent clauses when they are not connected with a coordinating conjunction.

Examples:

We worked in the yard; my muscles are sore.

I play tennis; Bob plays golf.

Use a semicolon to separate items in a series when the list contains commas.

Example:

This winter, snow fell in Minneapolis, MN; Bangor, ME; and Stowe, VT.

A **colon** is used to separate a list, introduce an important point, in the salutation of a business letter, and between numbers in time.

Examples:

Dear Dr. Adams:	**Salutation of a letter**
10:00 P.M.	**Time**
I hope in the twenty-first century we will have this disease wiped out: cancer.	**Introduce an important point**
I need to include: food for dinner, sleeping bags, tents, canoes, and clothes.	**Separate list**

Unit 13: Semicolons and Colons: *Exercise 1*

Directions: On the lines below, rewrite the sentences adding colons and semicolons where needed. Circle the punctuation that you add.

1. I can't wait to go to camp I will learn how to play tennis.

    _____

    _____

2. These are the three officers for student council Tom, Carol, and Steven.

    _____

    _____

3. I can think of only one word to describe this sunset magnificent.

    _____

    _____

4. You have a dentist appointment at 430 P.M.

    _____

    _____

5. Liz worked on her math homework I studied my French.

    _____

    _____

6. These are the supplies needed for class the book, a pencil, a pen, and paper.

    _____

    _____

7. Bill, when you build the rocket I want you to think of this be careful.

    _____

    _____

8. I have lived in Honolulu, HI St. Louis, MO Miami, FL and Quincy, IL.

    _____

    _____

Name: _____ Date: _____

Unit 13: Semicolons and Colons: *Exercise 2*

Directions: Rewrite the following letter using colons, semicolons, and commas correctly.

August 29 2000

Dear Mrs. Stevens

I am enclosing the information you asked for about the trip to New York New York on April 19 2000. The bill for your hotel room for April 19 2000 was $90.00. You checked in at 630 P.M. and stayed until 1045 A.M. on April 20 2000.

I do not have the charges for rooms in Baton Rouge Louisiana Columbus Ohio and Miami Florida. You will have to check with our main office.

Sincerely

Acme Travel Agency

_____

_____

_____

_____

_____

_____

_____

_____

_____

_____

Unit 14: Quotations: *Introduction*

Quotation marks are used to set off the exact words of the speaker. Quotation marks are written in pairs. One set is at the beginning of the quote, the other is at the end of the quote. When the speaker is at the beginning of the quotation, use a comma or the correct end punctuation and then the final quotation mark. If the speaker is at the end of the quotation, use a comma and then the final quotation mark.

Examples:

Ruis yelled, "Look out!"

"Is anyone ready for dinner?" Dad asked.

"How many of you brought your permission slips?" asked the teacher.

"I haven't read that book," Selena remarked.

"Stop!" shouted the police officer.

Allison answered, "There are twenty-six letters."

An **indirect quotation** is not the exact words of someone and is not set off by quotation marks.

Examples:

Mrs. Chen said the homework was due on Thursday.

Adam said it was in the closet.

Titles of short stories, essays, short poems, and song titles are enclosed in quotation marks.

Example:

We sang "Happy Birthday" at the party.

She wrote a poem titled "Tipsy, Topsy, Turvy."

Name: _____   Date: _____

Unit 14: Quotations: *Exercise 1*

Directions: Rewrite the following sentences using the correct punctuation.

1. When are we going to have the test Stephanie asked

    _____

2. Dennis yelled The dog ran away

    _____

3. Sarah pleaded Please let me copy the notes from last night

    _____

4. Please don't walk through my flower beds Mrs. Ames said.

    _____

5. Mrs. Dela Cruz announced There will be a test over this on Wednesday

    _____

    _____

6. When did you get your hair cut squealed Paula

    _____

7. Matt asked What new sites have you found on the Internet

    _____

8. Patricia shouted Wait for me

    _____

9. When are you going to bake cookies again moaned Jennifer

    _____

10. Duane said I don't think I'll be back for lunch

    _____

Name: _____ Date: _____

Unit 14: Quotations: *Exercise 2*

Directions: Rewrite the following sentences, putting quotation marks and proper punctuation where they are needed. Circle all added quotation marks.

1. Mom whistles The Star-Spangled Banner all the time.

   _____

2. Did anyone read Chapter 1: American Explorers?

   _____

3. I have memorized the poem Ode to Eggs.

   _____

4. I read an article in Time magazine, Life in the Sixties.

   _____

5. I love Disney's theme song When You Wish Upon a Star.

   _____

6. In science we had to read the chapter called Cell Division.

   _____

7. Stop the Sun is a story in our literature anthology.

   _____

8. Can you play Chopsticks on the piano?

   _____

9. The Gettysburg Address is one of the greatest speeches of all time.

   _____

   _____

10. Quinn wrote a poem called Roll Over Rover.

   _____

Name: _____   Date: _____

Unit 14: Quotations: *Exercise 3*

Directions: In the following sentences, write if it is a direct quotation or an indirect quotation. If it is a direct quotation, rewrite it as an indirect quotation. If it is an indirect quotation, rewrite it as a direct quotation.

1. "Who wants to go for ice cream?" yelled Mother. _____

    _____

    _____

2. Dad said he wanted someone to clean out the garage. _____

    _____

    _____

3. Ben said he had to stay after school. _____

    _____

    _____

4. "I am going to ride my bike to the park," said Peter. _____

    _____

    _____

5. Mrs. Jefferson replied, "Yes, you will need two tablespoons of honey." _____

    _____

    _____

6. Harriet asked if she could meet us at the bus. _____

    _____

    _____

7. Susan told me to meet her at the basketball game tonight. _____

    _____

    _____

8. Mrs. Rodriguez said, "Be quiet in the halls." _____

    _____

    _____

Name: _____   Date: _____

Unit 14: Quotations: *Tell Me More*

On the lines below, write a dialogue using one of the sentences from the previous page. Make sure you check the rules for using quotation marks.

_____

_____

_____

_____

_____

_____

_____

_____

_____

_____

_____

_____

_____

_____

_____

_____

_____

_____

Unit 15: Capitalization: *Introduction*

Capitalized letters are used to show that certain words and certain word groups are important. Capitalize words at the beginning of sentences. Capitalize all proper nouns and all proper adjectives. Capitalize titles of people and relatives. Capitalize holidays, important events, and periods of history.

Capitalize the beginning of sentences. The first letter of a sentence is always capitalized.

Examples:

What is your name?

She is going to camp today.

How old are you?

Mom asked, "Do you need a ride?"

Capitalize all proper nouns and proper adjectives.

A **proper noun** is the name of a specific person, place, or thing. A **proper adjective** is an adjective formed from a proper noun.

Examples:

Bart Starr	proper noun
February	proper noun
Spanish	proper adjective
France	proper noun
Monday	proper noun
American	proper adjective
Victorian	proper adjective

Unit 15: Capitalization: *Titles*

Capitalize the titles of people and relatives.

A title is used with a person's name to show respect or to show someone's position. Relatives' titles are also capitalized.

Examples:

Colonel Adams
Princess Leia
Aunt Lois
Mom

Hint: Don't capitalize words like mom, dad, uncle, grandmother, and so on, when used with a possessive pronoun.

Examples:

I asked my mom to drive.

We saw her grandmother.

Capitalize the titles president and vice president when they refer to the head of the government.

Examples:

George Washington was the first President of the United States.

The Vice President is taking over while the President has his operation.

Capitalize holidays, special events, and periods of history.

Examples:

Mother's Day	holiday
Veterans' Day	holiday
Election Day	special event
Dark Ages	period of history

Capitalize the first letter of all important words in the title of a book. Book titles are also underlined when they are hand-written.

Unit 15: Capitalization: *Abbreviations*

Abbreviations of proper nouns and adjectives are also capitalized.

Examples:

Sun.   Wed.   Jan.   Prof.   Mr.

Capitalize north, south, east, and west when you are naming a region, or in an address.

Examples:

My grandparents are traveling in the West.

Mr. Watkins likes the East.

I live at 1447 North Grant Avenue.

Capitalize titles of specific events.

Examples:

I would like to go to the World Series this year.

Have you ever been to the Rose Bowl?

Capitalize the names of the planets and other heavenly bodies.

Examples:

The closest planet is Venus.

The largest planet is Jupiter.

Hint: Sun, moon, and earth are usually not capitalized and never after the word the.

Capitalize the names of specific trains, planes, and ships. These names are also underlined.

Examples:

The Nautilus is a ship in the Navy.

Air Force One is the name of the President's plane.

Name: _____ Date: _____

Unit 15: Capitalization: *Exercise*

Directions: In the following sentences, add capital letters where needed. Put a line through the letter to be capitalized and write the capital letter above.

1. Do you live on east eighth street?

2. jody, will, kim, steven, and mitch are all in the choir.

3. do you go to dr. david miller?

4. the president and the vice president are traveling in europe.

5. did you get mother a mother's day card?

6. what did grandpa white ask you to do?

7. did you hear president clinton give the speech about the vietnam war?

8. admiral brown served on the uss stargazer.

9. can you come over on thurs. instead of fri.?

10. i am an eighth-grade student at butler middle school in waukesha, wi.

11. have you ever been to the world series or the superbowl?

12. we saw the headquarters of ibm corp.

13. missouri is one of the states u s grant lived in.

14. we saw the uss arizona when we went to honolulu hi.

15. one of my favorite authors is mark twain; he wrote a connecticut yankee in king
    arthur's court.

Name: _____   Date: _____

Unit 15: Capitalization: *Capitalizing Titles Exercise*

Directions: Rewrite each sentence with the correct capitalization and punctuation. Make sure you remember to underline the title.

1. my favorite book is brian's winter by gary paulsen.

    _____

2. harry potter and the sorcerer's stone is about a boy wizard.

    _____

3. do you use the encyclopedia brittanica from the library?

    _____

4. mrs. wallace said we had to use readers' guide to periodical literature.

    _____

    _____

5. have you ever read great expectations by charles dickens?

    _____

6. as a boy scout i subscribed to boys life magazine.

    _____

7. have you ever read the book the moved outers?

    _____

8. where did you put the encyclopedia americana?

    _____

9. president kennedy wrote a book called profiles in courage.

    _____

10. I've lost my copy of the adventures of tom sawyer.

    _____

Unit 16: Dictionary Use: *Introduction*

Dictionaries

A **dictionary** is used to look up the spelling and meaning of words. It also helps you find the pronunciation of the word, whether to capitalize the word or not, how many syllables are in the word, the part of speech, and synonyms and antonyms of the word. In order to do all of these things, it is important to know how to find the word you are looking for.

Dictionaries are in alphabetical order. At the top of each page are two **guide words** to help you find your word's page. These are the first and last words on that page. If the page has "chat" and "chin" at the top of the page, all of the words on that page are between those two words in alphabetical order.

Each word listed is called a **main entry word**. These are the words listed in alphabetical order on the page. The main entry word will be spelled correctly, capitalized correctly, and divided into syllables. Following the main entry word will be the part of speech and definition of the word. Sometimes words have one meaning and sometimes there are several. It is important to read all the definitions to see which one you need.

Glossaries

A **glossary** is a small dictionary found in the back of some books. It has an alphabetical listing, just like a dictionary, of words that are important to that book.

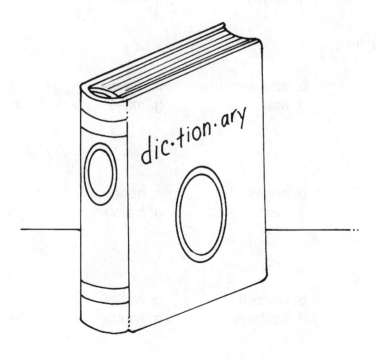

Name: _____ Date: _____

Unit 16: Dictionary Use: *Guide Words*

Directions: Look at the guide words and decide which words from the list will be on that page. Circle your answer.

1. gable / gainful

   a. gaggle   b. gaffe   c. gait   d. gaiety
   e. gabardine   f. gale   g. gage   h. gain

2. pass / paste

   a. passage   b. particle   c. pasture   d. passbook
   e. passion   f. partner   g. party   h. pastry

3. catcher / cauldron

   a. catch-up   b. cease   c. cavefish   d. cater
   e. caucus   f. cattle   g. cave   h. cauliflower

4. stiff / stir

   a. stilt   b. stock   c. stingray   d. stick
   e. stint   f. steward   g. stitch   h. stigma

5. material / maxim

   a. maze   b. mathematics c. mauve   d. maturity
   e. master   f. may   g. mate   h. matter

6. berth / bide

   a. beyond   b. beside   c. bevel   d. between
   e. bidding   f. best   g. billion   h. beret

7. wash / water

   a. watch   b. wasted   c. wallet   d. Washington
   e. wart   f. wattage   g. waste   h. waver

Name: _____ Date: _____

Unit 16: Dictionary Use: *Syllable Exercise*

Directions: Rewrite each of the following words into syllables. Leave spaces between each of the syllables. Use your dictionary for help.

1. widespread _____
2. blubber _____
3. believable _____
4. scrutiny _____
5. phenomenon _____
6. underneath _____
7. sorrowful _____
8. circumvent _____
9. waterway _____
10. princess _____
11. inhabited _____
12. uneventful _____
13. salary _____
14. innovative _____
15. worker _____

16. although _____
17. rejuvenate _____
18. introduction _____
19. contemplate _____
20. lovely _____
21. consequences _____
22. swimming _____
23. development _____
24. unable _____
25. dictionary _____
26. quietly _____
27. resentfully _____
28. supporter _____
29. exercise _____
30. adjustment _____

Unit 17: Writing: *Introduction*

Narrative Writing:

Narrative writing tells a story. It gives details of the event in the order in which they happen. A **personal narrative** tells a story of something that happened to the writer. An author can also write a narrative to report on an event that he or she watched. In a narrative, the most important parts are the details **who**, **what**, **when**, **where**, and **how**. The author must make the story a vivid picture in the reader's mind. The author needs to show, not tell, the audience what is happening.

Expository Writing:

Expository writing is used to inform or explain. Book reports, newspaper articles, and directions are all types of expository writing. Research papers and autobiographies are also expository writing. Travel brochures or books of instruction for computer games are expository writing, too. Expository writing is often done for writing assignments in school. Expository writing is true. The author does not put in his or her opinions.

Persuasive Writing:

In **persuasive writing**, the author is trying to convince or persuade someone to do something or to think the way the author does. Advertisements and political campaigns are persuasive writing. When you are trying to convince someone to let you do something, you are trying to persuade that person.

A persuasive writing piece has an introduction, a body, and a conclusion. The author grabs the reader's attention and sets out his or her argument in the **introduction**. In the body of the paper, reasons for the author's position are given and details supporting those reasons are provided. The **conclusion** sums up what the author has said and brings the paper to a close.

Name: _____ Date: _____

Unit 18: Narrative Writing: *Riding a Bike*

Directions: Remember when you learned to ride a bicycle? Think back to how you felt the first time you rode on your own. Who helped you learn to ride? Where were you? What did your first bike look like? Write a narrative describing the first time you learned to ride a bike. (If you are not a bike rider, write about another "first" you learned to do.)

_____

_____

_____

_____

_____

_____

_____

_____

_____

_____

_____

_____

_____

_____

_____

Name: _____   Date: _____

Unit 18: Narrative Writing: *A Special Time*

Directions: Think about a special time you spent with your mom, dad, brother, or sister. Describe that special time. Did you go somewhere special or do something special, or was it just the time you spent together that made it special? Write about that time, giving us details of the event.

_____

_____

_____

_____

_____

_____

_____

_____

_____

_____

_____

_____

_____

_____

_____

_____

_____

Name: _____ Date: _____

Unit 19: Expository Writing: *My Town*

Directions: Describe the town, city, or community in which you live. What does it look like? What is there to do? Who are your neighbors? Give as many details as possible.

_____

_____

_____

_____

_____

_____

_____

_____

_____

_____

_____

_____

_____

_____

_____

_____

_____

_____

_____

Name: _____ Date: _____

Unit 19: Expository Writing: *Space Travel*

Directions: What do you think it would be like to travel in space? How would you get there? Would you need a special space vehicle? Describe your adventure, using all the things you know about space and space travel.

_____

_____

_____

_____

_____

_____

_____

_____

_____

_____

_____

_____

_____

_____

_____

_____

_____

_____

Name: _____ Date: _____

Unit 20: Persuasive Writing: *If Elected I Would ...*

Directions: You are running for office in the seventh-grade student council. Decide in which office you would do well. Write a persuasive essay convincing the students that you would be the best candidate for that office.

_____

_____

_____

_____

_____

_____

_____

_____

_____

_____

_____

_____

_____

_____

_____

_____

_____

_____

Name: _____ Date: _____

Unit 20: Persuasive Writing: *The Party*

Directions: You would like to have a party at your house. Write an essay persuading your parents to allow you to have a party. Remember to include your reasons and supporting details.

_____

_____

_____

_____

_____

_____

_____

_____

_____

_____

_____

_____

_____

_____

_____

_____

_____

_____

_____

_____

Unit 21: Proofreading: *Introduction*

When you are finished with your writing, there is another step before you are ready to share your writing. You need to **proofread** your work.

Proofreading is going through your piece and looking at **spelling**, **mechanics**, **usage**, and **grammar**.

Spelling: Read the paper backwards to help catch misspelled words. This way, you will be looking at each word to check for spelling.

Mechanics: This is capitalization and punctuation. Are sentences and proper nouns capitalized? Do the sentences end with the correct mark? Has the writer used punctuation in dialogue correctly?

Usage: Are homonyms misused? Are all words used correctly?

Grammar: Check that pronouns and antecedents agree. Do the subjects and verbs agree? Are there run-on sentences or fragments?

You need to be very careful as you go through your paper and look for all the mistakes. Often, it is helpful to have a partner read your paper out loud to you so that you can hear how it actually sounds, making it easier to find mistakes. As you go through your paper or someone else's, there are special marks to use to make corrections. These are called **proofreading marks**.

Proofreading Marks: *A Guide*

Mark	Meaning	Example
⬭	Spelling	Sumbody ate all the ice cream.
≡	Capitalize	Have you ever been to indiana?
/	Lower case	My Grandpa fought in the war.
⊙	Add a period	I am going to the park today.
∧	Add a word	How many pieces of paper do I need?
∧	Add a comma	Jane, where are the markers?
∨	Add an apostrophe	Isn't Sally coming with us?
∨ ∨	Add quotation marks	Luis annouced, I am finished.
℘	Take out a letter, word, or phrase	I think you you are right.
∿	Reverse words or letters	Give the book me to.
→	Indent	On a cold January day.
¶	New paragraph	. . . we went to bed. The next day . . .

Name: _____ Date: _____

Unit 21: Proofreading: *Exercise 1*

Directions: Proofread each of the following sentences. Use the correct proofreading mark to show where a correction should be made.

1. Frederick joined the US. Army.

2. Where is mrs. jones?

3. I dont want to be late for school.

4. have yoou met this person before.

5. I need a book and and a pencil.

6. I think those are mine and Bens cookies.

7. Wear did you get the lemonade?

8. I think I am am getting better at tinnis.

9. I can't never get the lines straight without a ruler.

10. I wish thier were more holidays in the year.

11. Carol and me didnt see the movie.

12. I think I have more gumdrops then you.

13. Mary barb Sarah and me have been friends since sept 1996.

14. Wat day are you going on the tripp?

15. I done all my work and now I will reed.

Unit 21: Proofreading: *Exercise 2*

Directions: Proofread the following paragraph. Use the proofreading symbols for punctuation.

My mom and dad got me and my brother a dog this year. We were really happy. Its brown and red and will grow to be 75 lbs. We nammed her Rusty. She is a Airedale.

We were real happy untill we saw how much work it was to take care of her. The fisrt nite she was at our hous she wined all nite long. We put a clock in her cage with her to ty to keep her quiet but that didnt work. Me and my brohter took her to be with us. That kep her quiet.

Everyday we feed and water her and take her outside to play. She likes to play in the yard. Their she can run and run. There is only one problem with that she runs threw moms flowers and then we are all in trouble.

The other day she chased the cat around the room and the cat ran over the kitchen table to get away from Rusty. The only problem with that is to glasses of water were knocked over. We were all in trouble again.

Rusty also likes to get into the trash baskets and pull out the paper. She races all over the house with it. When mom sees that were all in trouble again.

Guss where we are going to be talking Rusty next week. We are goiing to obedience training. Hopefully that will keep us all out of trouble for ever.

Glossary of Terms

 Action Verb: A verb that shows physical or mental action

Adjective: Word that modifies a noun or a pronoun

Adverb: Word that modifies a verb, an adjective, or another adverb

Antecedent: The noun or pronoun that a pronoun refers to or replaces

Apostrophe: (') A punctuation mark used to show the omission of one or more letters and to show the possessive form of nouns

Appositives: Words that explain the noun they follow; they are set off from the rest of the sentence by commas

Article: An adjective that is used before a noun (*a, an,* and *the*)

 Body: The main part of a written composition

Business Letter: A formal letter written to compliment, complain, or request

 Capitalize: To write a letter of the alphabet in the upper case

Closing: The end of a letter

Colon: (:) Used to separate a list, introduce an important point, in the salutation of a business letter, and between numbers in time

Comma: (,) Punctuation mark used to separate words in a series or to show a pause

Common Noun: any person, place, or thing

Composition: A group of paragraphs to explain, persuade, or share an experience

Conclusion: The final paragraph of a composition that brings it to a close

Conjunction: A word that joins words or groups of words

Consonants: Letters of the alphabet that are not vowels

Coordinating Conjunction: Used to join similar words or groups of words

Correlative Conjunction: Conjunctions that are always used in pairs, such as *neither...nor*

 Declarative: A sentence that makes a statement and uses a period at the end

Demonstrative Pronoun: A pronoun used to point out a specific person, place, or thing

Dependent Clause: Has a subject and a verb but is not a complete thought

Dialogue: Conversation between two or more people

Direct Object: A noun or pronoun that follows an action verb and answers the questions What? or Whom?

Glossary of Terms

Exclamation Point: (!) Used at the end of a sentence to show excitement or surprise

Exclamatory: A sentence that shows excitement or surprise and uses an exclamation point at the end

Expository Writing: Writing used to inform or explain

Focus: The main idea of a paper

Friendly Letter: An informal letter to a friend, relative, or pen pal

Future Perfect Tense: Shows action that begins in the future and will be completed in the future

Future Tense: Shows action that will take place in the future

Glossary: A small dictionary found in the back of a book

Guide Words: The first and last words on a dictionary page, found at the top of each page

Heading: The address of the person writing a letter and the date

Helping Verb: A word that helps the main verb express action or state of being

Imperative: A sentence that makes a command and uses a period at the end

Indefinite Pronoun: A pronoun that does not refer to any specific person, place, or thing

Independent Clause: Has a subject and a verb and is a complete thought

Indirect Quotation: Not the exact words of someone; it is not set off by quotation marks

Inside Address: In a business letter, the address of the person and/or company to whom the letter is written

Interjection: A word or phrase used to express strong or sudden feeling, emotion, or surprise

Interrogative: A sentence that asks a question and has a question mark at the end

Interrogative Pronoun: A pronoun used to ask a question

Introduction: The part of a composition that tells the topic; usually the first paragraph

Lead: Grabs the attention of the reader; may be the first line or the first paragraph

Linking Verb: A word that links the subject to a noun or adjective in the predicate; it does not show action

Main Entry Word: Each entry in the dictionary

Narrative Writing: Writing that tells a story

Noun: A word that names a person, place, thing, or idea

Negative: A word such as *not, no,* or *never* that gives a negative meaning to a sentence

Glossary of Terms

Object of the Preposition: The noun or pronoun used with a preposition in a prepositional phrase

Object Pronoun: The object of the verb

Paragraph: A group of sentences that are about the same idea

Past Perfect Tense: Shows action that began in the past and was completed in the past

Past Tense: Shows action that happened in the past

Pen Pal: A friend made through exchanging letters

Period: (.) Punctuation used at the end of a sentence that is a statement (declarative) or a command (imperative)

Personal Pronoun: Refers to a specific person, place, or thing

Persuasive Writing: Writing used to convince or persuade someone to do something or to think in a certain way

Plural Noun: A noun that means more than one

Possessive Noun: A noun that shows ownership

Possessive Pronoun: A pronoun that shows ownership

Predicate: The sentence part that says something about the subject; it contains the verb or verb phrase

Preposition: A word that relates the noun or pronoun that follows it to some other word in the sentence

Prepositional Phrase: The group of words that includes the preposition, the object, and any words in between the two

Present Perfect Tense: Shows action that began in the past but continues in the present or is completed in the present

Present Tense: Shows action that is happening now

Pronoun: Word that takes the place of a noun

Proofreading: Checking writing for errors in spelling, punctuation, capitalization, and grammar

Proper Adjective: An adjective formed from a proper noun

Proper Noun: Names a specific person, place, or thing

Question Mark: (?) Punctuation used at the end of a sentence that asks a question (interrogative)

Quotation Marks: (" ") Punctuation used to set off words used in dialogue

Relative Pronoun: A pronoun that introduces a dependent clause that modifies a noun or pronoun

Return Address: The address of the person sending a letter; goes in the upper left-hand corner of the envelope

Glossary of Terms

Salutation: The greeting of a letter

Semicolon: (;) Used to indicate a longer pause than a comma, to link independent clauses not connected by a coordinating conjunction, and to separate items in a list when the list contains commas

Sentence: Group of words that expresses a complete thought

Sentence Fragment: Part of a sentence that does not express a complete thought

Signature: A letter writer's hand-written name

Simple Predicate: The verb or verb phrase in a sentence

Simple Sentence: Sentence that has only one subject and one verb

Simple Subject: The main noun in a sentence

Subject of a Sentence: Person, place, or thing that the sentence is about

Subject Pronoun: A word that takes the place of the subject of a sentence

Subordinate Conjunction: Joins a dependent and independent clause

Tense: Time expressed by a verb

Verb: Word that expresses action or a state of being

Vowels: "a," "e," "i," "o," "u," and sometimes "y"

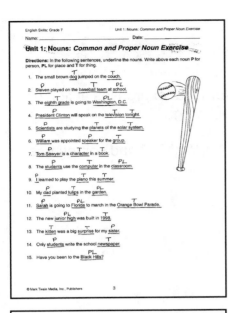

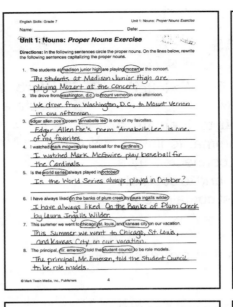

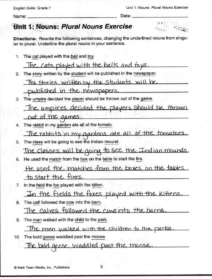

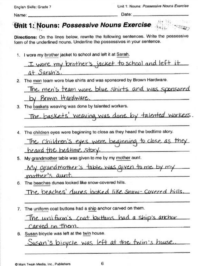

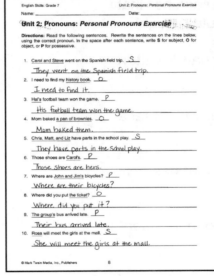

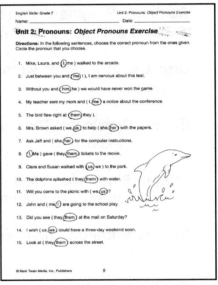

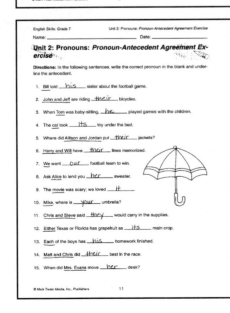

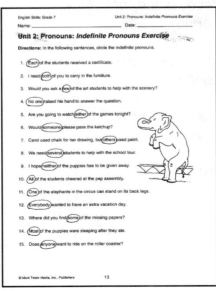

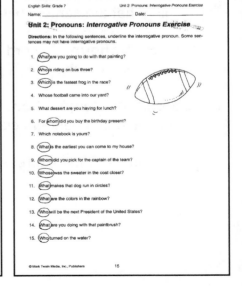

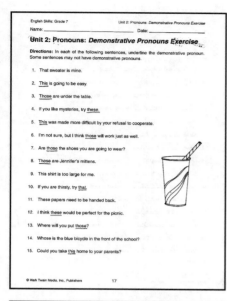

English Skills: Grade 7
Name: _____
Unit 2: Pronouns: *Demonstrative Pronouns Exercise*

Unit 2: Pronouns: *Demonstrative Pronouns Exercise*

Directions: In each of the following sentences, underline the demonstrative pronoun. Some sentences may not have demonstrative pronouns.

1. That sweater is mine.
2. <u>This</u> is going to be easy.
3. <u>Those</u> are under the table.
4. If you like mysteries, try <u>these</u>.
5. <u>This</u> was made more difficult by your refusal to cooperate.
6. I'm not sure, but I think <u>those</u> will work just as well.
7. Are <u>those</u> the shoes you are going to wear?
8. <u>These</u> are Jennifer's mittens.
9. This shirt is too large for me.
10. If you are thirsty, try <u>that</u>.
11. These papers need to be handed back.
12. I think <u>these</u> would be perfect for the picnic.
13. Where will you put <u>those</u>?
14. Whose is the blue bicycle in the front of the school?
15. Could you take <u>this</u> home to your parents?

© Mark Twain Media, Inc., Publishers   17

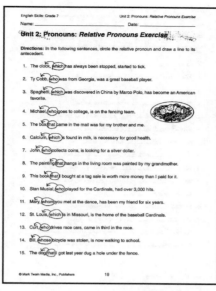

English Skills: Grade 7
Name: _____
Unit 2: Pronouns: *Relative Pronouns Exercise*

Unit 2: Pronouns: *Relative Pronouns Exercise*

Directions: In the following sentences, circle the relative pronoun and draw a line to its antecedent.

1. The clock, (which) has always been stopped, started to tick.
2. Ty Cobb, (who) was from Georgia, was a great baseball player.
3. Spaghetti, (which) was discovered in China by Marco Polo, has become an American favorite.
4. Michael, (who) goes to college, is on the fencing team.
5. The box (that) came in the mail was for my brother and me.
6. Calcium, (which) is found in milk, is necessary for good health.
7. John, (who) collects coins, is looking for a silver dollar.
8. The painting (that) hangs in the living room was painted by my grandmother.
9. This book (that) I bought at a tag sale is worth more money than I paid for it.
10. Stan Musial, (who) played for the Cardinals, had over 3,000 hits.
11. Mary, (whom) you met at the dance, has been my friend for six years.
12. St. Louis, (which) is in Missouri, is the home of the baseball Cardinals.
13. Curt, (who) drives race cars, came in third in the race.
14. Bill, (whose) bicycle was stolen, is now walking to school.
15. The dog (that) I got last year dug a hole under the fence.

© Mark Twain Media, Inc., Publishers   19

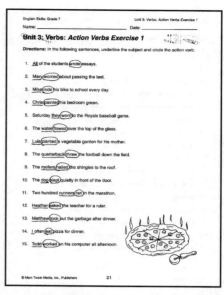

English Skills: Grade 7
Name: _____
Unit 3: Verbs: *Action Verbs Exercise 1*

Unit 3: Verbs: *Action Verbs Exercise 1*

Directions: In the following sentences, underline the subject and circle the action verb.

1. All of the students (wrote) essays.
2. Mary (worried) about passing the test.
3. Mike (rode) his bike to school every day.
4. Chris (painted) his bedroom green.
5. Saturday they (went) to the Royals baseball game.
6. The water (flowed) over the top of the glass.
7. Luis (planted) a vegetable garden for his mother.
8. The quarterback (threw) the football down the field.
9. The roofers (nailed) the shingles to the roof.
10. The dog (slept) quietly in front of the door.
11. Two hundred runners (ran) in the marathon.
12. Heather (asked) the teacher for a ruler.
13. Matthew (took) out the garbage after dinner.
14. I often (eat) pizza for dinner.
15. Todd (worked) on his computer all afternoon.

© Mark Twain Media, Inc., Publishers   21

English Skills: Grade 7
Name: _____ Date: _____
Unit 3: Verbs: *Action Verbs Exercise 2*

Unit 3: Verbs: *Action Verbs Exercise 2*

Directions: In the following sentences, underline the action verb and write T above it if it is transitive and I if it is intransitive.

1. The flowers <u>swayed</u> in the breeze. (I)
2. Barbara <u>typed</u> her report on the computer. (T)
3. Bill <u>played</u> football all Sunday afternoon. (T)
4. Bob and Carol <u>cleaned</u> the art room tables. (T)
5. All the students <u>signed</u> the get-well card for their teacher. (T)
6. During thunderstorms, our dog <u>hides</u>. (I)
7. Steve <u>thought</u> about the test. (I)
8. Pete <u>climbed</u> the rock wall. (T)
9. We <u>like</u> to race to the finish line. (T)
10. The crowd <u>yelled</u>. (I)
11. The campers <u>slept</u> near the campfire. (I)
12. The paint <u>ran</u> down the picture. (I)
13. My sister and I <u>share</u> a room. (T)
14. The cat <u>walked</u> out the door. (I)
15. The pilot <u>flew</u> the plane to Chicago. (T)

© Mark Twain Media, Inc., Publishers   22

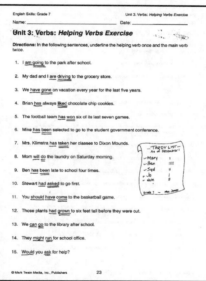

English Skills: Grade 7
Name: _____ Date: _____
Unit 3: Verbs: *Helping Verbs Exercise*

Unit 3: Verbs: *Helping Verbs Exercise*

Directions: In the following sentences, underline the helping verb once and the main verb twice.

1. I <u>am</u> <u>going</u> to the park after school.
2. My dad and I <u>are</u> <u>driving</u> to the grocery store.
3. We <u>have</u> <u>gone</u> on vacation every year for the last five years.
4. Brian <u>has</u> always <u>liked</u> chocolate chip cookies.
5. The football team <u>has</u> <u>won</u> six of its last seven games.
6. Mike <u>has</u> been <u>selected</u> to go to the student government conference.
7. Mrs. Klimstra <u>has</u> taken her classes to Dixon Mounds.
8. Mom <u>will</u> <u>do</u> the laundry on Saturday morning.
9. Ben <u>has</u> been <u>late</u> to school four times.
10. Stewart <u>had</u> <u>asked</u> to go first.
11. You <u>should</u> have <u>come</u> to the basketball game.
12. Those plants <u>had</u> <u>grown</u> to six feet tall before they were cut.
13. We <u>can</u> <u>go</u> to the library after school.
14. They <u>might</u> <u>run</u> for school office.
15. <u>Would</u> you <u>ask</u> for help?

© Mark Twain Media, Inc., Publishers   23

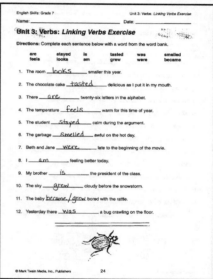

English Skills: Grade 7
Name: _____ Date: _____
Unit 3: Verbs: *Linking Verbs Exercise*

Unit 3: Verbs: *Linking Verbs Exercise*

Directions: Complete each sentence below with a word from the word bank.

| are | stayed | is | tasted | was | smelled |
| feels | looks | am | grew | were | became |

1. The room __looks__ smaller this year.
2. The chocolate cake __tasted__ delicious as I put it in my mouth.
3. There __are__ twenty-six letters in the alphabet.
4. The temperature __feels__ warm for this time of year.
5. The student __stayed__ calm during the argument.
6. The garbage __smelled__ awful on the hot day.
7. Beth and Jane __were__ late to the beginning of the movie.
8. I __am__ feeling better today.
9. My brother __is__ the president of the class.
10. The sky __grew__ cloudy before the snowstorm.
11. The baby __became / grew__ bored with the rattle.
12. Yesterday there __was__ a bug crawling on the floor.

© Mark Twain Media, Inc., Publishers   24

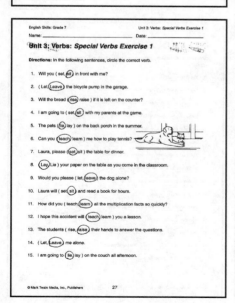

English Skills: Grade 7
Name: _____ Date: _____
Unit 3: Verbs: *Special Verbs Exercise 1*

Unit 3: Verbs: *Special Verbs Exercise 1*

Directions: In the following sentences, circle the correct verb.

1. Will you (set, (sit)) in front with me?
2. (Let, (Leave)) the bicycle pump in the garage.
3. Will the bread ((rise), raise) if it is left on the counter?
4. I am going to (set, (sit)) with my parents at the game.
5. The pets ((lie), lay) on the back porch in the summer.
6. Can you ((teach), learn) me how to play tennis?
7. Laura, please ((set), sit) the table for dinner.
8. ((Lay), Lie) your paper on the table as you come in the classroom.
9. Would you please (let, (leave)) the dog alone?
10. Laura will (set, (sit)) and read a book for hours.
11. How did you (teach, (learn)) all the multiplication facts so quickly?
12. I hope this accident will ((teach), learn) you a lesson.
13. The students (rise, (raise)) their hands to answer the questions.
14. (Let, (Leave)) me alone.
15. I am going to ((lie), lay) on the couch all afternoon.

© Mark Twain Media, Inc., Publishers   27

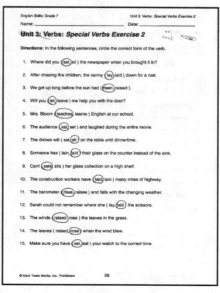

English Skills: Grade 7
Name: _____ Date: _____
Unit 3: Verbs: *Special Verbs Exercise 2*

Unit 3: Verbs: *Special Verbs Exercise 2*

Directions: In the following sentences, circle the correct form of the verb.

1. Where did you ((set), sit) the newspaper when you brought it in?
2. After chasing the children, the nanny ((lay), laid) down for a rest.
3. We got up long before the sun had ((risen), raised).
4. Will you ((let), leave) me help you with the door?
5. Mrs. Bloom ((teaches), learns) English at our school.
6. The audience ((sat), set) and laughed during the entire movie.
7. The dishes will (set, (sit)) on the table until dinnertime.
8. Someone has (lain, (laid)) their glass on the counter instead of the sink.
9. Cam ((sets), sits) her glass collection on a high shelf.
10. The construction workers have ((laid), lain) many miles of highway.
11. The barometer ((rises), raises) and falls with the changing weather.
12. Sarah could not remember where she (lay, (laid)) the scissors.
13. The winds ((raised), rose) the leaves in the grass.
14. The leaves (raised, (rose)) when the wind blew.
15. Make sure you have ((set), sat) your watch to the correct time.

© Mark Twain Media, Inc., Publishers   28

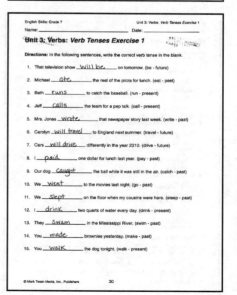

English Skills: Grade 7
Name: _____ Date: _____
Unit 3: Verbs: *Verb Tenses Exercise 1*

Unit 3: Verbs: *Verb Tenses Exercise 1*

Directions: In the following sentences, write the correct verb tense in the blank.

1. That television show __will be__ on tomorrow. (be - future)
2. Michael __ate__ the rest of the pizza for lunch. (eat - past)
3. Beth __runs__ to catch the baseball. (run - present)
4. Jeff __calls__ the team for a pep talk. (call - present)
5. Mrs. Jones __wrote__ that newspaper story last week. (write - past)
6. Carolyn __will travel__ to England next summer. (travel - future)
7. Cars __will drive__ differently in the year 2310. (drive - future)
8. I __paid__ one dollar for lunch last year. (pay - past)
9. Our dog __caught__ the ball while it was still in the air. (catch - past)
10. We __went__ to the movies last night. (go - past)
11. We __slept__ on the floor when my cousins were here. (sleep - past)
12. I __drink__ two quarts of water every day. (drink - present)
13. They __swam__ in the Mississippi River. (swim - past)
14. You __made__ brownies yesterday. (make - past)
15. You __walk__ the dog tonight. (walk - present)

© Mark Twain Media, Inc., Publishers   30

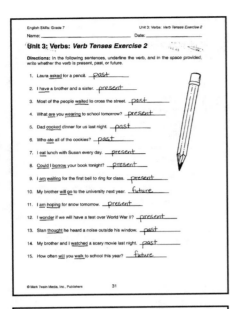

English Skills: Grade 7 — Unit 3: Verbs: Verb Tenses Exercise 2

Name: _____ Date: _____

Unit 3: Verbs: Verb Tenses Exercise 2

Directions: In the following sentences, underline the verb, and in the space provided, write whether the verb is present, past, or future.

1. Laura asked for a pencil. past
2. I have a brother and a sister. present
3. Most of the people waited to cross the street. past
4. What are you wearing to school tomorrow? present
5. Dad cooked dinner for us last night. past
6. Who ate all of the cookies? past
7. I eat lunch with Susan every day. present
8. Could I borrow your book tonight? present
9. I am waiting for the first bell to ring for class. present
10. My brother will go to the university next year. future
11. I am hoping for snow tomorrow. present
12. I wonder if we will have a test over World War II? present
13. Stan thought he heard a noise outside his window. past
14. My brother and I watched a scary movie last night. past
15. How often will you walk to school this year? future

© Mark Twain Media, Inc., Publishers   31

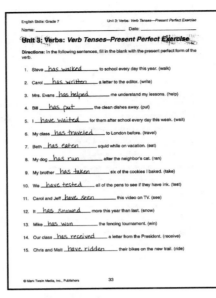

English Skills: Grade 7 — Unit 3: Verbs: Verb Tenses—Present Perfect Exercise

Name: _____ Date: _____

Unit 3: Verbs: Verb Tenses–Present Perfect Exercise

Directions: In the following sentences, fill in the blank with the present perfect form of the verb.

1. Steve has walked to school every day this year. (walk)
2. Carol has written a letter to the editor. (write)
3. Mrs. Evans has helped me understand my lessons. (help)
4. Bill has put the clean dishes away. (put)
5. I have waited for them after school every day this week. (wait)
6. My class has traveled to London before. (travel)
7. Beth has eaten squid while on vacation. (eat)
8. My dog has run after the neighbor's cat. (ran)
9. My brother has taken six of the cookies I baked. (take)
10. We have tested all of the pens to see if they have ink. (test)
11. Carol and Jeff have seen this video on TV. (see)
12. It has snowed more this year than last. (snow)
13. Mike has won the fencing tournament. (win)
14. Our class has received a letter from the President. (receive)
15. Chris and Matt have ridden their bikes on the new trail. (ride)

© Mark Twain Media, Inc., Publishers   33

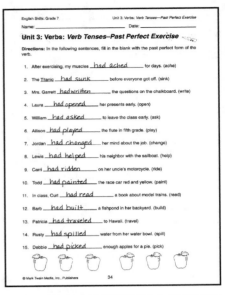

English Skills: Grade 7 — Unit 3: Verbs: Verb Tenses—Past Perfect Exercise

Name: _____ Date: _____

Unit 3: Verbs: Verb Tenses–Past Perfect Exercise

Directions: In the following sentences, fill in the blank with the past perfect form of the verb.

1. After exercising, my muscles had ached for days. (ache)
2. The Titanic had sunk before everyone got off. (sink)
3. Mrs. Garrett had written the questions on the chalkboard. (write)
4. Laura had opened her presents early. (open)
5. William had asked to leave the class early. (ask)
6. Allison had played the flute in fifth grade. (play)
7. Jordan had changed her mind about the job. (change)
8. Lewis had helped his neighbor with the sailboat. (help)
9. Carri had ridden on her uncle's motorcycle. (ride)
10. Todd had painted the race car red and yellow. (paint)
11. In class, Curt had read a book about model trains. (read)
12. Barb had built a fishpond in her backyard. (build)
13. Patricia had traveled to Hawaii. (travel)
14. Rusty had spilled water from his water bowl. (spill)
15. Debbie had picked enough apples for a pie. (pick)

© Mark Twain Media, Inc., Publishers   34

English Skills: Grade 7 — Unit 3: Verbs: Verb Tenses—Future Perfect Exercise

Name: _____ Date: _____

Unit 3: Verbs: Verb Tenses–Future Perfect Exercise

Directions: In the following sentences, fill in the blank with the future perfect form of the verb.

1. By the time I get to school, I will have walked three miles today. (walk)
2. We will have made the decorations before the dance. (make)
3. Barbara will have finished her project by the due date. (finish)
4. Michael will have learned a lot from the chess master. (learn)
5. As a joke, they will have worn matching outfits all week. (wear)
6. Scott will have participated in every spelling bee at school. (participate)
7. By the end of the year, I will have saved one hundred dollars. (save)
8. Jane will have told me at the end of the week who she likes. (tell)
9. Matt will have looked in every classroom for his notebook. (look)
10. Laura will have read the most books in our class. (read)
11. By the end of the day, Mike will have cleaned his room. (clean)
12. Alex will have practiced his piano piece many times. (practice)
13. If you eat this one too, you will have eaten all of my birthday treats. (eat)

© Mark Twain Media, Inc., Publishers   35

English Skills: Grade 7 — Unit 3: Verbs: Verb Tenses—Perfect Tense Review

Name: _____ Date: _____

Unit 3: Verbs: Verb Tenses–Perfect Tense Review

Directions: In the blank following the sentence, write if the verb is present perfect, past perfect, or future perfect tense.

1. I will have read every book in the library by the end of summer. future perfect
2. The action movie has broken the record for stunts in one movie. present perfect
3. Where have you left your coat and mittens? present perfect
4. Mack has gone back to get his jacket. present perfect
5. The dishes had been left on the counter. past perfect
6. Next month, Hal will have been in charge of recycling for the past two years. future perfect
7. Barb will have finished knitting the sweater by Christmas. future perfect
8. Have you brought the music for the party? present perfect
9. Brian had run that race before. past perfect
10. By the time you get my letter, I will have been gone two weeks. future perfect
11. I have been swimming since I was three years old. present perfect
12. Where have you put the salt and pepper? present perfect
13. I will have paid for all the decorations myself. future perfect
14. Wendy has known David for a long time. present perfect
15. Bill will have left on vacation by this time tomorrow. future perfect

© Mark Twain Media, Inc., Publishers   36

English Skills: Grade 7 — Unit 4: Adjectives: Adjectives Exercise

Name: _____ Date: _____

Unit 4: Adjectives: Adjectives Exercise

Directions: In the following sentences, underline the adjectives and draw a line from the adjective to the noun it modifies.

1. The cool air felt good after being in the hot sun.
2. After the bright sun sets, the sky turns a dark purple black.
3. Where are you going with that old, brown couch?
4. The happy students played with the antique toys.
5. May I have a large, cold glass of water?
6. Some people keep their important papers in a locked cabinet.
7. Curt took his big, black motorcycle to the two-wheeler show.
8. Beth took the yellow sweater with the pink flowers to the garage sale.
9. The tall, blue vase held long-stemmed, red roses.
10. Four chocolate chip cookies were left on the green napkin.
11. Those old newspapers can be thrown in the recycling bin.
12. While it snowed, we caught fluffy flakes in our open mouths.
13. The angry cat hissed at the big, black dog.
14. The tropical, blue water sparkled in the bright sunlight.
15. I would like to have a sandwich with American cheese for my lunch.

© Mark Twain Media, Inc., Publishers   39

English Skills: Grade 7 — Unit 4: Adjectives: Proper Adjectives Exercise

Name: _____ Date: _____

Unit 4: Adjectives: Proper Adjectives Exercise

Directions: Rewrite the following sentences capitalizing the proper adjectives. Underline the proper adjectives once and all other adjectives twice.

1. The italian newspaper reported water fountains in Rome would be turned off.
   The Italian newspaper reported water fountains in Rome would be turned off.
2. I would like to stay in a beautiful french chateau with a large garden.
   I would like to stay in a beautiful French chateau with a large garden.
3. Do you think that mexican food uses hot spices?
   Do you think that Mexican food uses hot spices?
4. We saw some beautiful chinese artwork in the american museum.
   We saw some beautiful Chinese artwork in the American museum.
5. The canadian hockey star was going to play on an american team.
   The Canadian hockey star was going to play on an American team.
6. My uncle likes german food, but I prefer to eat italian food.
   My uncle likes German food, but I prefer to eat Italian food.
7. We import irish sweaters, swiss chocolates, and english dishes.
   We import Irish sweaters, Swiss chocolates, and English dishes.
8. The brazilian rain forests are being saved by conservation groups.
   The Brazilian rain forests are being saved by conservation groups.

© Mark Twain Media, Inc., Publishers   40

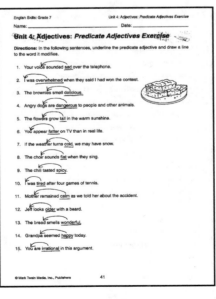

English Skills: Grade 7 — Unit 4: Adjectives: Predicate Adjectives Exercise

Name: _____ Date: _____

Unit 4: Adjectives: Predicate Adjectives Exercise

Directions: In the following sentences, underline the predicate adjective and draw a line to the word it modifies.

1. Your voice sounded sad over the telephone.
2. I was overwhelmed when they said I had won the contest.
3. The brownies smell delicious.
4. Angry dogs are dangerous to people and other animals.
5. The flowers grow tall in the warm sunshine.
6. You appear fatter on TV than in real life.
7. If the weather turns cold, we may have snow.
8. The choir sounds flat when they sing.
9. The chili tasted spicy.
10. I was tired after four games of tennis.
11. Mother remained calm as we told her about the accident.
12. Jeff looks older with a beard.
13. The bread smells wonderful.
14. Grandpa seemed happy today.
15. You are irrational in this argument.

© Mark Twain Media, Inc., Publishers   41

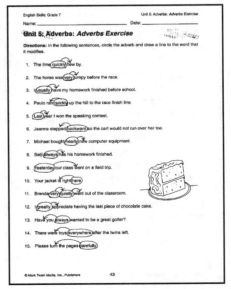

English Skills: Grade 7 — Unit 5: Adverbs: Adverbs Exercise

Name: _____ Date: _____

Unit 5: Adverbs: Adverbs Exercise

Directions: In the following sentences, circle the adverb and draw a line to the word that it modifies.

1. The time quickly flew by.
2. The horse was very jumpy before the race.
3. I usually have my homework finished before school.
4. Paulo ran quickly up the hill to the race finish line.
5. Last year I won the speaking contest.
6. Jeanne stepped backward so the cart would not run over her toe.
7. Michael bought nearly new computer equipment.
8. Seiji always has his homework finished.
9. Yesterday your class went on a field trip.
10. Your jacket is right here.
11. Brenda very quietly went out of the classroom.
12. I greatly appreciate having the last piece of chocolate cake.
13. Have you always wanted to be a great golfer?
14. There were toys everywhere after the twins left.
15. Please turn the pages carefully.

© Mark Twain Media, Inc., Publishers   43

Unit 5: Adverbs: *Using Negatives Exercise*

Directions: In the following sentences, circle the correct word in the parentheses to make the sentences negative.

1. No one ((ever) never) said you could stay up late tonight?
2. Sarah hasn't said ((anything) nothing).
3. The splinter was so little you (couldn't, (could)) not see it.
4. You don't act ((anything) nothing) like your older sister.
5. Do you want ((nothing) anything) from the grocery store?
6. The kittens weren't ((anywhere) nowhere) in the barn.
7. I saw (anything, (nothing)) that looked strange in the puzzle.
8. I ((could) couldn't) not find the mistake in the knitting.
9. (Weren't, (Were)) none of the books on the back shelf?
10. The quiz didn't have (no, (any)) easy answers.
11. Haven't you ((ever) never) eaten chocolate-covered ants?
12. We don't want ((any)) extra people on the committee.
13. I (couldn't, (could)) never learn to paint.
14. Wouldn't (nobody, (anybody)) join the fencing team?
15. There wasn't (no, (any)) money to pay for the pizzas and the ice cream.

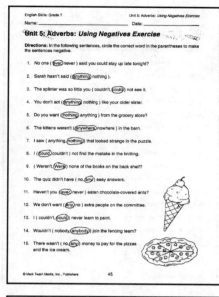

45

Unit 6: Adjectives and Adverbs: *Comparison Adjectives Exercise*

Directions: Fill in the blank with the correct form of the adjective in parentheses.

1. My sister is **taller** than yours. (tall)
2. Mrs. Cornwell has the **prettiest** voice in the choir. (pretty)
3. This is the **most beautiful** dress I have ever seen. (beautiful)
4. My dad is **more cautious** than my grandpa. (cautious)
5. My dog is the **sloppiest** eater. (sloppy)
6. Claudia is the **fastest** runner in our room. (fast)
7. This test is **harder** than last week's test. (hard)
8. Steven is **bigger** than Jeff. (big)
9. This is the **most important** day of my life. (important)
10. Jeff is the **shortest** boy playing basketball. (short)
11. My cat is **more beautiful** than that one. (beautiful)
12. That actor played the **most convincing** blind person in the movie. (convincing)
13. Turn in your **most complete** writing assignment. (complete)
14. May I have a **larger** brownie today, please? (large)
15. Where is the **warmest** sweater I have? (warm)

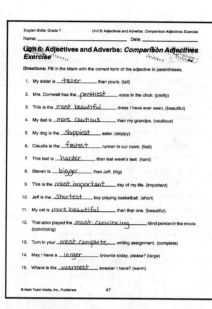

47

Unit 6: Adjectives and Adverbs: *Comparison Adverbs Exercise*

Directions: Fill in the blank with the correct form of the adverb in parentheses.

1. Richard can run **the fastest** of all the track stars. (fast)
2. I completed the test **more successfully** than my lab partner. (successfully)
3. John, you acted **more responsibly** than Jeff during the fire drill. (responsibly)
4. Louise raced **more quickly** than Steve. (quickly)
5. My kite flew **higher** today than yesterday. (high)
6. The pitcher who pitches **more successfully** wins the game. (successfully)
7. To win the prize in speech, you must speak **more distinctly** than the other contestants. (distinctly)
8. Why do the days leading up to vacation pass **more slowly** than the other days? (slowly)
9. Keith learned the music **more easily** than Robert. (easily)
10. You need to dig **deeper** to find water. (deep)
11. Luis read **more confidently** this year than last. (confidently)
12. This train runs **more speedily** than the steam engine. (speedily)
13. The bell rang **later** today than yesterday. (late)
14. My mother stays up **the latest** of everyone in the family. (late)
15. To win a game, you must practice **the hardest** of all the participants. (hard)

48

Unit 6: Adjectives and Adverbs: *Good, Bad, Well, and Badly Exercise*

Directions: In the sentences below, circle the correct word for the sentence. In the space provided, write if it is an adjective or an adverb.

1. Beth always feels (good, (well)) after jogging. **adjective**
2. Those brownies taste ((good) well). **adjective**
3. After a week, the fish tasted ((bad) badly). **adjective**
4. Carlos's CD player looks really ((good) well). **adjective**
5. Mrs. Jones said I did (good, (well)) on the test. **adverb**
6. Your new spaghetti recipe tastes ((bad) badly). **adjective**
7. Sue fell and hurt her elbow (bad, (badly)). **adverb**
8. Jane felt ((bad) badly) about missing the appointment. **adjective**
9. Cool water feels ((good) well) on a hot day. **adjective**
10. If you don't feel (good, (well)), then you should go home. **adverb**
11. The game was played (bad, (badly)) and they lost. **adverb**
12. Our team played (bad, (badly)) in last night's game. **adverb**
13. You need to swim (good, (well)) to pass the swim test. **adverb**
14. Peter's choice for dinner was a ((good) well) one. **adjective**
15. I hope all the plans for the dance go (good, (well)). **adverb**
16. Our team ran (bad, (badly)) in the race, but we still won. **adverb**

50

Unit 7: Prepositions: *Object of Prepositions Exercise*

Directions: In the following sentences, circle the preposition and draw an arrow to its object.

1. My berth (on) the ship is (below) the water line.
2. I like to read (about) the English monarchy.
3. The waves wash (over) us.
4. There is a cornfield (behind) our house.
5. When it started to rain, I ran (inside) the house.
6. I received a letter (from) my pen pal.
7. We browsed (through) the book department.
8. I fixed dinner (by) myself.
9. My school is (near) the fire department.
10. The bowling ball rolled (between) the pins.
11. The speeding car stopped (against) the telephone pole.
12. I would run away (from) a bear.
13. The picture is hung (over) the table.
14. I put the tulip bulbs (among) the evergreen bushes.
15. Nancy slid (down) the snowy hill.

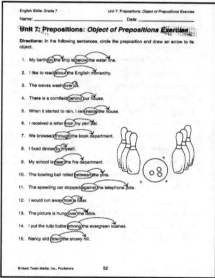

52

Unit 7: Prepositions: *Prepositional Phrases Exercise*

Directions: In the following sentences, circle each prepositional phrase. Draw one line under the preposition and draw two lines under the object of the preposition in each phrase.

1. The apple (in the bottom) (of the basket) had a worm.
2. My classroom's number is (over the door).
3. The racer (with the fastest time) will win the race.
4. The dart that lands (within the bull's-eye) gets the most points.
5. You must walk (between the cones) to pass the obstacle course.
6. I walked (up the hill).
7. My dog is not to go (beyond the fence).
8. My brother gave me a book (of magic tricks).
9. I put the ribbon (around the present).
10. The river ran (toward the sea).
11. I put the bologna (between the two bread slices).
12. I like to learn (about American Indians).
13. I got an autograph (from a famous baseball player).
14. The ball bounced (near the net).
15. Check (under the table) (for your pencil).

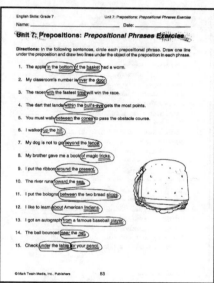

53

Unit 7: Prepositions: *Preposition or Adverb? Exercise*

Directions: In the following sentences, decide if the underlined word is an adverb or a preposition, and in the space provided, write preposition or adverb.

1. I like to read outside. **adverb**
2. The flower box is underneath the window. **preposition**
3. Zack walked out. **adverb**
4. Curt fell in. **adverb**
5. They live near the lake. **preposition**
6. Do you live between the school and my house? **preposition**
7. Barbara worked on them all afternoon. **preposition**
8. The rabbits played behind the bushes. **preposition**
9. The wind blew against the windows. **preposition**
10. The submarine ran beneath the water. **preposition**
11. Can we run across? **adverb**
12. There were people throughout. **adverb**
13. Please get out. **adverb**
14. The kids hung around the fire house. **preposition**
15. We drove along the coastline. **preposition**

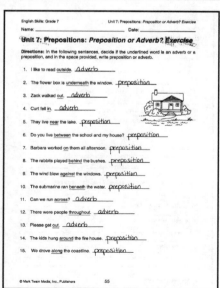

55

Unit 7: Prepositions: *Special Prepositions Exercise 1*

Directions: In the following sentences, circle the correct prepositions.

1. I sat (between, (among)) the children when the story was read.
2. ((Between) Among) you and me, I think this test will be easy.
3. (Beside, (Besides)) the two of us, who is going to the play?
4. Please put the crackers ((beside) besides) the bread in the pantry.
5. Look at that tulip growing ((between) among) the two roses.
6. The disagreement was (between, (among)) those three students.
7. What do you have to eat (beside, (besides)) peanut butter and jelly?
8. We are going to divide our money (between, (among)) several charities.
9. I couldn't get ((between) among) the two lines in the hall.
10. I sat ((beside) besides) Mr. Sanchez in the school assembly.
11. There was no one left in the classroom (beside, (besides)) Mrs. Jones.
12. How can you choose (between, (among)) all the great prizes?
13. Would you stand ((between) among) Ling and Rita?
14. I found a dollar in my jeans (beside, (besides)) the two dollars you have.
15. Could you all get along (between, (among)) yourselves?

58

Unit 7: Prepositions: *Special Prepositions Exercise 2*

Directions: In the following sentences, circle the correct word or words that best complete each sentence.

1. The marble rolled ((off) off of) the table and onto the floor.
2. Tomorrow I need to be ready to go (at about, (at)) 7:45.
3. Where are you taking the ((package) package to)?
4. Mary ((could have) could of) made the cake for the party.
5. We will be home ((at) at about) 4:00.
6. I never know where I will find my ((book) book at).
7. The water ran (off of, (off)) the new raincoat.
8. I (should of, (should have)) had an "A" on that paper.
9. We (could of, (could have)) won the game with one more run.
10. Have you seen where Jim ((is) is at)?
11. The train will arrive (at about, (at)) 12:30.
12. The yarn rolled (off of, (off)) the chair and onto the floor.
13. I must ((have) have of) added these two numbers incorrectly.
14. I need the book; will you show me where it ((is) is at)?
15. The musical starts ((about) at about) 8:00.

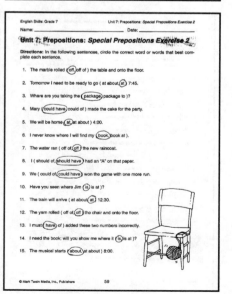

59

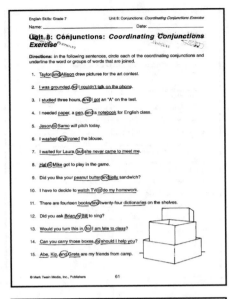

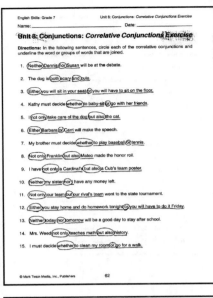

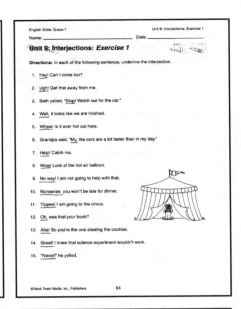

Unit 8: Conjunctions: Coordinating Conjunctions Exercise

Directions: In the following sentences, circle each of the coordinating conjunctions and underline the word or groups of words that are joined.

1. Taylor and Allison drew pictures for the art contest.
2. I was grounded, so I couldn't talk on the phone.
3. I studied three hours, and I got an "A" on the test.
4. I needed paper, a pen, and a notebook for English class.
5. Jason or Samo will pitch today.
6. I washed and ironed the blouse.
7. I waited for Laura, but she never came to meet me.
8. Hal or Mike got to play in the game.
9. Did you like your peanut butter and jelly sandwich?
10. I have to decide to watch TV or do my homework.
11. There are fourteen books and twenty-four dictionaries on the shelves.
12. Did you ask Brian or Bill to sing?
13. Would you turn this in, for I am late to class?
14. Can you carry those boxes, or should I help you?
15. Abe, Kip, and Greta are my friends from camp.

Unit 8: Conjunctions: Correlative Conjunctions Exercise

Directions: In the following sentences, circle each of the correlative conjunctions and underline the word or groups of words that are joined.

1. Neither Dennis nor Susan will be at the debate.
2. The dog is both scary and cute.
3. Either you will sit in your seat or you will have to sit on the floor.
4. Kathy must decide whether to baby-sit or go with her friends.
5. Not only take care of the dog but also the cat.
6. Either Barbara or Carri will make the speech.
7. My brother must decide whether to play baseball or tennis.
8. Not only Franklin but also Mateo made the honor roll.
9. I have not only a Cardinal's but also a Cub's team poster.
10. Neither my sister nor I have any money left.
11. Not only our team but our rival's team went to the state tournament.
12. Either you stay home and do homework tonight or you will have to do it Friday.
13. Neither today nor tomorrow will be a good day to stay after school.
14. Mrs. Weed not only teaches math but also history.
15. I must decide whether to clean my room or go for a walk.

Unit 9: Interjections: Exercise 1

Directions: In each of the following sentence, underline the interjection.

1. Hey! Can I come too?
2. Ugh! Get that away from me.
3. Beth yelled, "Stop! Watch out for the car."
4. Well, it looks like we are finished.
5. Whew! Is it ever hot out here.
6. Grandpa said, "My, the cars are a lot faster than in my day."
7. Help! Catch me.
8. Wow! Look at the hot air balloon.
9. No way! I am not going to help with that.
10. Nonsense, you won't be late for dinner.
11. Yippee! I am going to the circus.
12. Oh, was that your book?
13. Aha! So you're the one stealing the cookies.
14. Great! I knew that science experiment wouldn't work.
15. "Never!" he yelled.

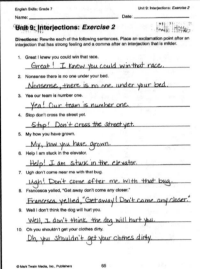

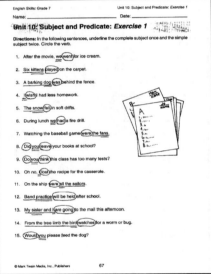

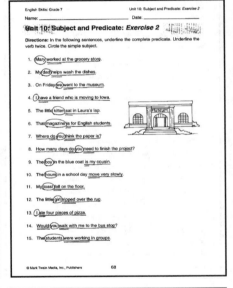

Unit 9: Interjections: Exercise 2

Directions: Rewrite each of the following sentences. Place an exclamation point after an interjection that has strong feeling and a comma after an interjection that is milder.

1. Great I knew you could win that race.
   Great! I knew you could win that race.
2. Nonsense there is no one under your bed.
   Nonsense, there is no one under your bed.
3. Yea our team is number one.
   Yea! Our team is number one.
4. Stop don't cross the street yet.
   Stop! Don't cross the street yet.
5. My how you have grown.
   My, how you have grown.
6. Help I am stuck in the elevator.
   Help! I am stuck in the elevator.
7. Ugh don't come near me with that bug.
   Ugh! Don't come after me with that bug.
8. Francesca yelled, "Get away don't come any closer."
   Francesca yelled, "Get away! Don't come any closer."
9. Well I don't think the dog will hurt you.
   Well, I don't think the dog will hurt you.
10. Oh you shouldn't get your clothes dirty.
    Oh, you shouldn't get your clothes dirty.

Unit 10: Subject and Predicate: Exercise 1

Directions: In the following sentences, underline the complete subject once and the simple subject twice. Circle the verb.

1. After the movie, we went for ice cream.
2. Six kittens played on the carpet.
3. A barking dog was behind the fence.
4. I wish I had less homework.
5. The snow fell in soft drifts.
6. During lunch we had a fire drill.
7. Watching the baseball game were the fans.
8. Did you leave your books at school?
9. Do you think this class has too many tests?
10. Oh no, I lost the recipe for the casserole.
11. On the ship were all the sailors.
12. Band practice will be held after school.
13. My sister and I are going to the mall this afternoon.
14. From the tree limb the bird watches for a worm or bug.
15. Would you please feed the dog?

Unit 10: Subject and Predicate: Exercise 2

Directions: In the following sentences, underline the complete predicate. Underline the verb twice. Circle the simple subject.

1. Mary worked at the grocery store.
2. My dad helps wash the dishes.
3. On Friday we went to the museum.
4. I have a friend who is moving to Iowa.
5. The little kitten sat in Laura's lap.
6. That magazine is for English students.
7. Where do you think the paper is?
8. How many days do you need to finish the project?
9. The boy in the blue coat is my cousin.
10. The hours in a school day move very slowly.
11. My toast fell on the floor.
12. The little girl tripped over the rug.
13. I ate four pieces of pizza.
14. Would you walk with me to the bus stop?
15. The students were working in groups.

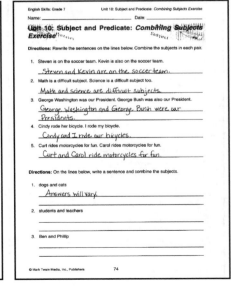

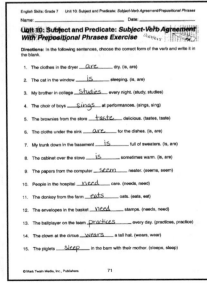

Unit 10: Subject and Predicate: Subject-Verb Agreement Exercise

Directions: In the following sentences, underline the subject of the sentence, then circle the form of the verb given in the parentheses that agrees with the subject of the sentence.

1. The cats (hunts, hunt) for mice.
2. She (walks, walk) to school for exercise.
3. Mr. Ricardo (teaches, teach) Spanish.
4. An airplane (soars, soar) over our heads.
5. The dishes (is, are) in the cupboard.
6. Mrs. Yung (talks, talk) with her students every day.
7. The students (plans, plan) the carnival.
8. They (eats, eat) lunch together.
9. Here (is, are) the papers you were looking for.
10. Luis (sits, sit) in the front of the auditorium.
11. Svetlana (takes, take) piano lessons.
12. The program (is, are) not correct for the performance.
13. The dog (acts, act) friendly.
14. The cake (looks, look) delicious.
15. The dog (barks, bark) at the rabbit in the yard.

Unit 10: Subject and Predicate: Subject-Verb Agreement With Prepositional Phrases Exercise

Directions: In the following sentences, choose the correct form of the verb and write it in the blank.

1. The clothes in the dryer __are__ dry. (is, are)
2. The cat in the window __is__ sleeping. (is, are)
3. My brother in college __studies__ every night. (study, studies)
4. The choir of boys __sings__ at performances. (sings, sing)
5. The brownies from the store __taste__ delicious. (tastes, taste)
6. The cloths under the sink __are__ for the dishes. (is, are)
7. My trunk down in the basement __is__ full of sweaters. (is, are)
8. The cabinet over the stove __is__ sometimes warm. (is, are)
9. The papers from the computer __seem__ neater. (seems, seem)
10. People in the hospital __need__ care. (needs, need)
11. The donkey from the farm __eats__ oats. (eats, eat)
12. The envelopes in the basket __need__ stamps. (needs, need)
13. The ballplayer on the team __practices__ every day. (practices, practice)
14. The clown at the circus __wears__ a tall hat. (wears, wear)
15. The piglets __sleep__ in the barn with their mother. (sleeps, sleep)

Unit 10: Subject and Predicate: Combining Subjects Exercise

Directions: Rewrite the sentences on the lines below. Combine the subjects in each pair.

1. Steven is on the soccer team. Kevin is also on the soccer team.
   Steven and Kevin are on the soccer team.
2. Math is a difficult subject. Science is a difficult subject too.
   Math and science are difficult subjects.
3. George Washington was our President. George Bush was also our President.
   George Washington and George Bush were our Presidents.
4. Cindy rode her bicycle. I rode my bicycle.
   Cindy and I rode our bicycles.
5. Curt rides motorcycles for fun. Carol rides motorcycles for fun.
   Curt and Carol ride motorcycles for fun.

Directions: On the lines below, write a sentence and combine the subjects.

1. dogs and cats
   Answers will vary.
2. students and teachers
3. Ben and Phillip

Page 75 — Unit 10: Subject and Predicate: *Combining Predicates Exercise*

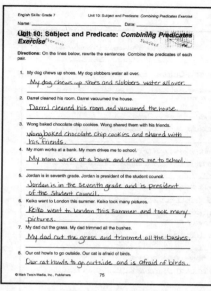

Directions: On the lines below, rewrite the sentences. Combine the predicates of each pair.

1. My dog chews up shoes. My dog slobbers water all over.
   My dog chews up shoes and slobbers water all over.

2. Darrel cleaned his room. Darrel vacuumed the house.
   Darrel cleaned his room and vacuumed the house.

3. Wong baked chocolate chip cookies. Wong shared them with his friends.
   Wong baked chocolate chip cookies and shared with his friends.

4. My mom works at a bank. My mom drives me to school.
   My mom works at a bank and drives me to school.

5. Jordan is in seventh grade. Jordan is president of the student council.
   Jordan is in the seventh grade and is president of the student council.

6. Keiko went to London this summer. Keiko took many pictures.
   Keiko went to London this summer and took many pictures.

7. My dad cut the grass. My dad trimmed all the bushes.
   My dad cut the grass and trimmed all the bushes.

8. Our cat howls to go outside. Our cat is afraid of birds.
   Our cat howls to go outside and is afraid of birds.

Page 76 — Unit 10: Subject and Predicate: *Combining Sentences Exercise*

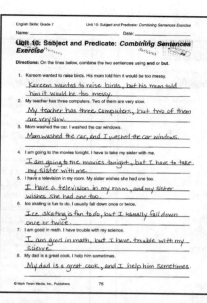

Directions: On the lines below, combine the two sentences using *and* or *but*.

1. Kareem wanted to raise birds. His mom told him it would be too messy.
   Kareem wanted to raise birds, but his mom told him it would be too messy.

2. My teacher has three computers. Two of them are very slow.
   My teacher has three computers, but two of them are very slow.

3. Mom washed the car. I washed the car windows.
   Mom washed the car, and I washed the car windows.

4. I am going to the movies tonight. I have to take my sister with me.
   I am going to the movies tonight, but I have to take my sister with me.

5. I have a television in my room. My sister wishes she had one too.
   I have a television in my room, and my sister wishes she had one too.

6. Ice skating is fun to do. I usually fall down once or twice.
   Ice skating is fun to do, but I usually fall down once or twice.

7. I am good in math. I have trouble with my science.
   I am good in math, but I have trouble with my science.

8. My dad is a great cook. I help him sometimes.
   My dad is a great cook, and I help him sometimes.

Page 78 — Unit 11: Clauses: *Exercise 1*

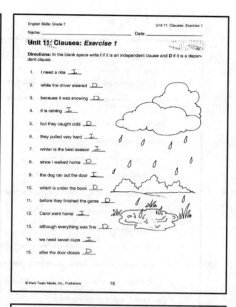

Directions: In the blank space write I if it is an independent clause and D if it is a dependent clause.

1. I need a ride   *I*
2. while the driver steered   *D*
3. because it was snowing   *D*
4. it is raining   *I*
5. but they caught cold   *D*
6. they pulled very hard   *I*
7. winter is the best season   *I*
8. since I walked home   *D*
9. the dog ran out the door   *I*
10. which is under the book   *D*
11. before they finished the game   *D*
12. Carol went home   *I*
13. although everything was fine   *D*
14. we need seven cups   *I*
15. after the door closes   *D*

Page 79 — Unit 11: Clauses: *Exercise 2*

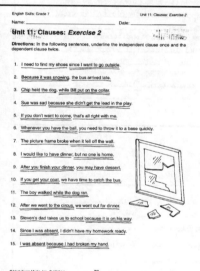

Directions: In the following sentences, underline the independent clause once and the dependent clause twice.

1. I need to find my shoes since I want to go outside.
2. Because it was snowing, the bus arrived late.
3. Chip held the dog, while Bill put on the collar.
4. Sue was sad because she didn't get the lead in the play.
5. If you don't want to come, that's all right with me.
6. Whenever you have the ball, you need to throw it to a base quickly.
7. The picture frame broke when it fell off the wall.
8. I would like to have dinner, but no one is home.
9. After you finish your dinner, you may have dessert.
10. If you get your coat, we have time to catch the bus.
11. The boy walked while the dog ran.
12. After we went to the circus, we went out for dinner.
13. Steven's dad takes us to school because it is on his way.
14. Since I was absent, I didn't have my homework ready.
15. I was absent because I had broken my hand.

Page 82 — Unit 12: Commas: *Commas With Dates Exercise*

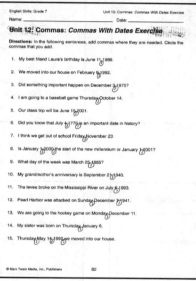

Directions: In the following sentences, add commas where they are needed. Circle the commas that you add.

1. My best friend Laura's birthday is June 11, 1989.
2. We moved into our house on February 9, 1992.
3. Did something important happen on December 3, 1975?
4. I am going to a baseball game Thursday, October 14.
5. Our class trip will be June 15, 2001.
6. Did you know that July 4, 1776 is an important date in history?
7. I think we get out of school Friday, November 23.
8. Is January 1, 2000 the start of the new millennium or January 1, 2001?
9. What day of the week was March 25, 1885?
10. My grandmother's anniversary is September 21, 1940.
11. The levee broke on the Mississippi River on July 6, 1993.
12. Pearl Harbor was attacked on Sunday, December 7, 1941.
13. We are going to the hockey game on Monday, December 11.
14. My sister was born on Thursday, January 6.
15. Thursday, May 14, 1992 we moved into our house.

Page 83 — Unit 12: Commas: *Exercise 1*

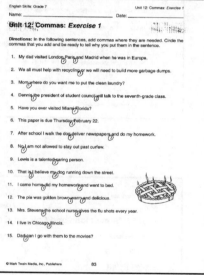

Directions: In the following sentences, add commas where they are needed. Circle the commas that you add and be ready to tell why you put them in the sentence.

1. My dad visited London, Paris, and Madrid when he was in Europe.
2. We all must help with recycling, or we will need to build more garbage dumps.
3. Mom, where do you want me to put the clean laundry?
4. Dennis, the president of student council, will talk to the seventh-grade class.
5. Have you ever visited Miami, Florida?
6. This paper is due Thursday, February 22.
7. After school I walk the dog, deliver newspapers, and do my homework.
8. No, I am not allowed to stay out past curfew.
9. Lewis is a talented, caring person.
10. That is, I believe, my dog running down the street.
11. I came home, did my homework, and went to bed.
12. The pie was golden brown, warm, and delicious.
13. Mrs. Stevens, the school nurse, gives the flu shots every year.
14. I live in Chicago, Illinois.
15. Dad, can I go with them to the movies?

Page 84 — Unit 12: Commas: *Exercise 2*

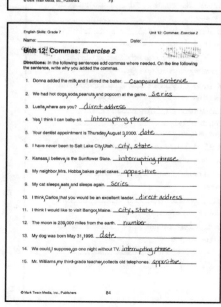

Directions: In the following sentences add commas where needed. On the line following the sentence, write why you added the commas.

1. Donna added the milk, and I stirred the batter.   *Compound sentence*
2. We had hot dogs, soda, peanuts, and popcorn at the game.   *Series*
3. Luella, where are you?   *direct address*
4. Yes, I think I can baby-sit.   *interrupting phrase*
5. Your dentist appointment is Thursday, August 3, 2000.   *date*
6. I have never been to Salt Lake City, Utah.   *city, state*
7. Kansas, I believe, is the Sunflower State.   *interrupting phrase*
8. My neighbor, Mrs. Hobbs, bakes great cakes.   *appositive*
9. My cat sleeps, eats, and sleeps again.   *Series*
10. I think, Carlos, that you would be an excellent leader.   *direct address*
11. I think I would like to visit Bangor, Maine.   *city, state*
12. The moon is 239,000 miles from the earth.   *number*
13. My dog was born May 31, 1996.   *date*
14. We could, I suppose, go one night without TV.   *interrupting phrase*
15. Mr. Williams, my third-grade teacher, collects old telephones.   *appositive*

Page 85 — Unit 12: Commas: *Independent Clause Exercise*

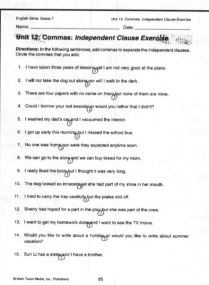

Directions: In the following sentences, add commas to separate the independent clauses. Circle the commas that you add.

1. I have taken three years of lessons, yet I am not very good at the piano.
2. I will not take the dog out alone, nor will I walk in the dark.
3. There are four papers with no name on them, but none of them are mine.
4. Could I borrow your red sweater, or would you rather that I didn't?
5. I washed my dad's car, and I vacuumed the interior.
6. I got up early this morning, but I missed the school bus.
7. No one was home, nor were they expected anytime soon.
8. We can go to the store, and we can buy bread for my mom.
9. I really liked the book, but I thought it was very long.
10. The dog looked so innocent, yet she had part of my shoe in her mouth.
11. I tried to carry the tray carefully, but the plates slid off.
12. Sherry had hoped for a part in the play, but she was part of the crew.
13. I want to get my homework done, and I want to see the TV movie.
14. Would you like to write about a holiday, or would you like to write about summer vacation?
15. Sun Li has a sister, and I have a brother.

Page 86 — Unit 12: Commas: *Separating Dependent Clauses From Independent Clauses Exercise*

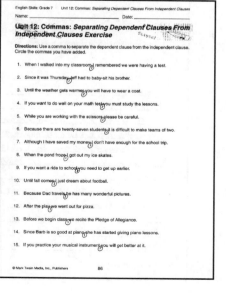

Directions: Use a comma to separate the dependent clause from the independent clause. Circle the commas that you have added.

1. When I walked into my classroom, I remembered we were having a test.
2. Since it was Thursday, Jeff had to baby-sit his brother.
3. Until the weather gets warmer, you will have to wear a coat.
4. If you want to do well on your math test, you must study the lessons.
5. While you are working with the scissors, please be careful.
6. Because there are twenty-seven students, it is difficult to make teams of two.
7. Although I have saved my money, I don't have enough for the school trip.
8. When the pond froze, I got out my ice skates.
9. If you want a ride to school, you need to get up earlier.
10. Until fall comes, I just dream about football.
11. Because Dad travels, he has many wonderful pictures.
12. After the play, we went out for pizza.
13. Before we begin class, we recite the Pledge of Allegiance.
14. Since Barb is so good at piano, she has started giving piano lessons.
15. If you practice your musical instrument, you will get better at it.

Name: _____ Date: _____

Unit 12: Commas: *Prepositional Phrases Exercise*

Directions: In the following sentences, add commas to make the sentence correct. Circle the commas you have added.

1. After dinner, we all went for a walk.
2. In the middle of my sentence, John interrupted.
3. Under the living room couch, my homework lay.
4. After all the practices, I still didn't make the football team.
5. On the corner of 12th Street and Elm Street, the public library stands.
6. In the back of the classroom, the goldfish bowl sat.
7. During my speech, I forgot to show the graph.
8. In spite of all Karen's effort, the fund raiser was a hundred dollars short.
9. With the addition of Lincoln and Kurt, we will have a great team.
10. In the middle of the classroom, a cart with all our dictionaries sits.
11. Across the river, a small village is located.
12. During basketball time-outs, the cheerleaders cheer.
13. In the morning, Maria and Luis will walk to school.
14. After 10:00 P.M., my mom won't let me answer the phone.
15. At the end of the school day, all the clubs meet.

Name: _____ Date: _____

Unit 13: Semicolons and Colons: *Exercise 1*

Directions: On the lines below, rewrite the sentences adding colons and semicolons where needed. Circle the punctuation that you add.

1. I can't wait to go to camp I will learn how to play tennis.
   I can't wait to go to camp; I will learn how to play tennis.
2. These are the three officers for student council Tom, Carol, and Steven.
   These are the three officers for student council: Tom, Carol, and Steven.
3. I can think of only one word to describe this sunset magnificent.
   I can think of only one word to describe this sunset: magnificent.
4. You have a dentist appointment at 430 P.M.
   You have a dentist appointment at 4:30 P.M.
5. Liz worked on her math homework I studied my French.
   Liz worked on her math homework; I studied my French.
6. These are the supplies needed for class the book, a pencil, a pen, and paper.
   These are the supplies needed for class: the book, a pencil, a pen, and paper.
7. Bill, when you build the rocket I want you to think of this be careful.
   Bill, when you build the rocket, I want you to think of this: be careful.
8. I have lived in Honolulu, HI St. Louis, MO Miami, FL and Quincy, IL.
   I have lived in Honolulu, HI; St. Louis, MO; Miami, FL; and Quincy, IL.

Name: _____ Date: _____

Unit 13: Semicolons and Colons: *Exercise 2*

Directions: Rewrite the following letter using colons, semicolons, and commas correctly.

August 29 2000

Dear Mrs. Stevens

     I am enclosing the information you asked for about the trip to New York New York on April 19 2000. The bill for your hotel room for April 19 2000 was $90.00. You checked in at 630 P.M. and stayed until 1045 A.M. on April 20 2000.

     I do not have the charges for rooms in Baton Rouge Louisiana Columbus Ohio and Miami Florida. You will have to check with our main office.

Sincerely

Acme Travel Agency

August 29, 2000
Dear Mrs. Stevens:
     I am enclosing the information you asked for about the trip to New York, New York, on April 19, 2000. The bill for your hotel room for April 19, 2000 was $90.00. You checked in at 6:30 P.M. and stayed until 10:45 A.M. on April 20, 2000.
     I do not have the charges for rooms in Baton Rouge, Louisiana; Columbus, Ohio; and Miami, Florida. You will have to check with our main office.
Sincerely,
Acme Travel Agency

Name: _____ Date: _____

Unit 14: Quotations: *Exercise 1*

Directions: Rewrite the following sentences using the correct punctuation.

1. When are we going to have the test Stephanie asked
   "When are we going to have the test?" Stephanie asked.
2. Dennis yelled The dog ran away
   Dennis yelled, "The dog ran away!"
3. Sarah pleaded Please let me copy the notes from last night
   Sarah pleaded, "Please let me copy the notes from last night."
4. Please don't walk through my flower beds Mrs. Ames said.
   "Please don't walk through my flower beds," Mrs. Ames said.
5. Mrs. Dela Cruz announced There will be a test over this on Wednesday
   Mrs. Dela Cruz announced, "There will be a test over this on Wednesday."
6. When did you get your hair cut squealed Paula
   "When did you get your hair cut?" squealed Paula.
7. Matt asked What new sites have you found on the Internet
   Matt asked, "What new sites have you found on the Internet?"
8. Patricia shouted Wait for me
   Patricia shouted, "Wait for me!"
9. When are you going to bake cookies again moaned Jennifer
   "When are you going to bake cookies again?" moaned Jennifer.
10. Duane said I don't think I'll be back for lunch
    Duane said, "I don't think I'll be back for lunch."

English Skills: Grade 7
Name: _____ Date: _____
Unit 14: Quotations: Exercise 2

Unit 14: Quotations: *Exercise 2*

Directions: Rewrite the following sentences, putting quotation marks and proper punctuation where they are needed. Circle all added quotation marks.

1. Mom whistles The Star-Spangled Banner all the time.
   Mom whistles "The Star-Spangled Banner" all the time.

2. Did anyone read Chapter 1: American Explorers?
   Did anyone read Chapter 1: "American Explorers"?

3. I have memorized the poem Ode to Eggs.
   I have memorized the poem "Ode to Eggs."

4. I read an article in Time magazine, Life in the Sixties.
   I read an article in *Time* magazine, "Life in the Sixties."

5. I love Disney's theme song When You Wish Upon a Star.
   I love Disney's theme song "When You Wish Upon a Star."

6. In science we had to read the chapter called Cell Division.
   In science we had to read the chapter called "Cell Division."

7. Stop the Sun is a story in our literature anthology.
   "Stop the Sun" is a story in our literature anthology.

8. Can you play Chopsticks on the piano?
   Can you play "Chopsticks" on the piano?

9. The Gettysburg Address is one of the greatest speeches of all time.
   "The Gettysburg Address" is one of the greatest speeches of all time.

10. Quinn wrote a poem called Roll Over Rover.
    Quinn wrote a poem called "Roll Over Rover."

English Skills: Grade 7
Name: _____ Date: _____
Unit 14: Quotations: Exercise 3

Unit 14: Quotations: *Exercise 3*

Directions: In the following sentences, write if it is a direct quotation or an indirect quotation. If it is a direct quotation, rewrite it as an indirect quotation. If it is an indirect quotation, rewrite it as a direct quotation.

1. "Who wants to go for ice cream?" yelled Mother. Direct Quote.
   Mother asked who wanted to go for ice cream.

2. Dad said he wanted someone to clean out the garage. Indirect Quote.
   Dad said, "I want someone to clean out the garage."

3. Ben said he had to stay after school. Indirect Quote.
   Ben said, "I had to stay after school."

4. "I am going to ride my bike to the park," said Peter. Direct Quote.
   Peter said he is going to ride his bike in the park.

5. Mrs. Jefferson replied, "Yes, you will need two tablespoons of honey." Direct Quote.
   Mrs. Wyatt said you will need two tablespoons of honey.

6. Harriet asked if she could meet us at the bus. Indirect Quote.
   Harriet asked, "Could I meet you at the bus?"

7. Susan told me to meet her at the basketball game tonight. Indirect Quote.
   Susan said, "Meet me at the basketball game tonight."

8. Mrs. Rodriguez said, "Be quiet in the halls." Direct Quote.
   Mrs. Rodriguez said to be quiet in the halls.

English Skills: Grade 7
Name: _____ Date: _____
Unit 15: Capitalization: Exercise

Unit 15: Capitalization: *Exercise*

Directions: In the following sentences, add capital letters where needed. Put a line through the letter to be capitalized and write the capital letter above.

1. Do you live on east eighth street? (E, E, S)
2. Jody, will, kim, steven, and mitch are all in the choir. (J, W, K, S, M)
3. do you go to dr. david miller? (D, D, D, M)
4. the president and the vice president are traveling in europe. (T, P, V, P, E)
5. did you get mother a mother's day card? (D, M, M, D)
6. what did grandpa white ask you to do? (W, G, W)
7. did you hear president clinton give the speech about the vietnam war? (D, P, C, V, W)
8. admiral brown served on the uss stargazer. (A, B, USS S)
9. can you come over on thurs. instead of fri.? (C, T, F)
10. I am an eighth-grade student at butler middle school in waukesha, wi. (I, B, M, S, W, WI)
11. have you ever been to the world series or the superbowl? (H, W, S, S)
12. we saw the headquarters of ibm corp. (W, IBM C)
13. missouri is one of the states u.s. grant lived in. (M, U S G)
14. we saw the uss arizona when we went to honolulu hi. (W, USS A, H, HI)
15. one of my favorite authors is mark twain; he wrote a connecticut yankee in king arthur's court. (O, M, T, A, C, Y, K, A, C)

English Skills: Grade 7
Name: _____ Date: _____
Unit 15: Capitalization: Capitalizing Titles Exercise

Unit 15: Capitalization: *Capitalizing Titles Exercise*

Directions: Rewrite each sentence with the correct capitalization and punctuation. Make sure you remember to underline the title.

1. my favorite book is brian's winter by gary paulsen.
   My favorite book is Brian's Winter by Gary Paulsen.

2. harry potter and the sorcerer's stone is about a boy wizard.
   Harry Potter and The Sorcerer's Stone is about a boy wizard.

3. do you use the encyclopedia brittanica from the library?
   Do you use the Encyclopedia Brittanica from the library?

4. mrs. wallace said we had to use readers' guide to periodical literature.
   Mrs. Wallace said we had to use Readers' Guide to Periodical Literature.

5. have you ever read great expectations by charles dickens?
   Have you ever read Great Expectations by Charles Dickens?

6. as a boy scout i subscribed to boys life magazine.
   As a boy scout I subscribed to Boys Life magazine.

7. have you ever read the book the moved outers?
   Have you ever read the book The Moved Outers?

8. where did you put the encyclopedia americana?
   Where did you put the Encyclopedia Americana?

9. president kennedy wrote a book called profiles in courage.
   President Kennedy wrote a book called Profiles In Courage.

10. I've lost my copy of the adventures of tom sawyer.
    I've lost my copy of The Adventures of Tom Sawyer.

English Skills: Grade 7   Unit 16: Dictionary Use: *Guide Words*

Name: _____ Date: _____

Unit 16: Dictionary Use: *Guide Words*

Directions: Look at the guide words and decide which words from the list will be on that page. Circle your answer.

1. gable / gainful

   (a.) gaggle   (b.) gaffe   c. gait   (d.) gaiety
   e. gabardine   f. gale   (g.) gage   (h.) gain

2. pass / paste

   (a.) passage   b. particle   c. pasture   (d.) passbook
   (e.) passion   f. partner   g. party   h. pastry

3. catcher / cauldron

   (a.) catch-up   b. cease   c. cavefish   (d.) cater
   (e.) caucus   (f.) cattle   g. cave   (h.) cauliflower

4. stiff / stir

   (a.) stilt   b. stock   (c.) stingray   d. stick
   (e.) stint   f. steward   g. stitch   (h.) stigma

5. material / maxim

   a. maze   (b.) mathematics   (c.) mauve   (d.) maturity
   e. master   f. may   g. mate   (h.) matter

6. berth / bide

   (a.) beyond   (b.) beside   (c.) bevel   (d.) between
   (e.) bidding   (f.) best   g. billion   h. beret

7. wash / water

   (a.) watch   (b.) wasted   c. wallet   (d.) Washington
   e. wart   f. wattage   (g.) waste   h. waver

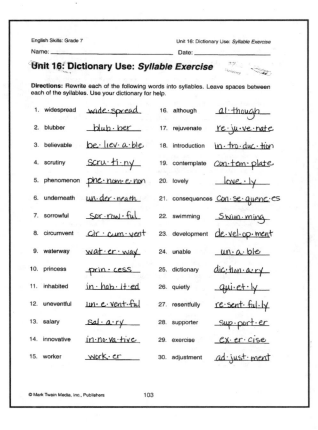

English Skills: Grade 7   Unit 16: Dictionary Use: *Syllable Exercise*

Name: _____ Date: _____

Unit 16: Dictionary Use: *Syllable Exercise*

Directions: Rewrite each of the following words into syllables. Leave spaces between each of the syllables. Use your dictionary for help.

1. widespread   wide·spread   16. although   al·though
2. blubber   blub·ber   17. rejuvenate   re·ju·ve·nate
3. believable   be·liev·a·ble   18. introduction   in·tro·duc·tion
4. scrutiny   scru·ti·ny   19. contemplate   con·tem·plate
5. phenomenon   phe·nom·e·non   20. lovely   love·ly
6. underneath   un·der·neath   21. consequences   con·se·quenc·es
7. sorrowful   sor·row·ful   22. swimming   swim·ming
8. circumvent   cir·cum·vent   23. development   de·vel·op·ment
9. waterway   wat·er·way   24. unable   un·a·ble
10. princess   prin·cess   25. dictionary   dic·tion·a·ry
11. inhabited   in·hab·it·ed   26. quietly   qui·et·ly
12. uneventful   un·e·vent·ful   27. resentfully   re·sent·ful·ly
13. salary   sal·a·ry   28. supporter   sup·port·er
14. innovative   in·no·va·tive   29. exercise   ex·er·cise
15. worker   work·er   30. adjustment   ad·just·ment

English Skills: Grade 7   Unit 21: Proofreading: *Exercise 1*

Name: _____ Date: _____

Unit 21: Proofreading: *Exercise 1*

Directions: Proofread each of the following sentences. Use the correct proofreading mark to show where a correction should be made.

1. Frederick joined the U.S. Army.
2. Where is mrs. jones?
3. I dont want to be late for school.
4. have you met this person before?
5. I need a book and and a pencil.
6. I think those are mine and Bens cookies.
7. Wear did you get the lemonade?
8. I think I am am getting better at tinnis.
9. I can't never get the lines straight without a ruler.
10. I wish thier were more holidays in the year.
11. Carol and me didnt see the movie.
12. I think I have more gumdrops then you.
13. Mary barb Sarah and me have been friends since sept, 1996.
14. Wat day are you going on the tripp?
15. I done all my work and now I will reed.

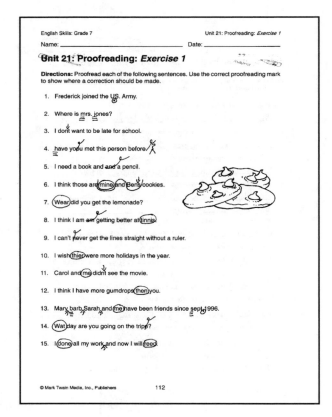

English Skills: Grade 7   Unit 21: Proofreading: *Exercise 2*

Unit 21: Proofreading: *Exercise 2*

Directions: Proofread the following paragraph. Use the proofreading symbols for punctuation.

My mom and dad got me and my brother a dog this year. We were really happy. Its brown and red and will grow to be 75 lbs. We named her Rusty. She is a Airedale.

We were real happy untill we saw how much work it was to take care of her. The fisrt nite she was at our house she wined all nite long. We put a clock in her cage with her to ty to keep her quiet but that didnt work. Me and my brohter took her to be with us. That kep her quiet.

Everyday we feed and water her and take her outside to play. She likes to play in the yard. Their she can run and run. There is only one problem with that she runs threw moms flowers and then we are all in trouble.

The other day she chased the cat around the room and the cat ran over the kitchen table to get away from Rusty. The only problem with that is to was glasses of water were knocked over. We were all in trouble again.

Rusty also likes to get into the trash baskets and pull out the paper. She races all over the house with it. When mom sees that were all in trouble again.

Guss where we are going to be talking Rusty next week. We are going to obedience training. Hopefully that will keep us all out of trouble for ever.
